A China Primer: An Introduction To A Culture And A Neighbour

A China Primer:
An Introduction To A Culture And A Neighbour

G. S. Iyer

Vij Books India Pvt Ltd
New Delhi (India)

Indian Council of World Affairs
Sapru House, New Delhi

A China Primer: An Introduction To A Culture And A Neighbour
First Published in India in 2016

Published by

Vij Books India Pvt Ltd
(Publishers, Distributors & Importers)
2/19, Ansari Road
Delhi – 110 002
Phones: 91-11-43596460, 91-11-47340674
Fax: 91-11-47340674
e-mail: vijbooks@rediffmail.com
web : www.vijbooks.com

ISBN: 978-93-85563-24-9 (Hardback)
ISBN: 978-93-85563-04-1 (Paperback)

Contents

Introduction: Why Another Book on China?

Do we need another book on China when so much has been written about that country? Don't we know all that we have to about its economic achievements and its future greatness, which, we are assured, is so obvious and beyond debate? That could be the first question asked about this book. Yes, there are several reasons to write another book, a book that describes China from our, a really Indian, point of view.

What is attempted here is an essay that would tell the reader about China's history and culture; its habits of behaviour that emerge from that history and culture; how these characteristics impel the way that country works; and how it conducted itself and does so now. The attempt is to integrate the flow of China's history with current affairs. Such an attempt is necessary because most of China scholarship in its comprehensive best is developed in Western countries. Is that good or not from our perspective? The great historian and philosopher of history Arnold J. Toynbee opens his magnum opus, *A Study of History*, with the statement that 'historians generally illustrate rather than correct the ideas of the communities within which they live and work'.[1] All scholarship originates from the points of view and interests of the society that produces that scholarship and its results are invariably tinged with the assumptions and beliefs that are predominant in that society and, if that scholarship is effective and of high quality, it will promote the larger aims and agenda of that culture. It goes without saying that Western scholarship on China cannot be an exception; it is not based on universally accepted foundations, but reflects both the specific biases and the broader objectives of that society vis-a-vis China.

It also follows that, while we in India could use such scholarship as is available – and it is abundant and rich in quality – we have an obligation to develop our own point of view and draw our own conclusions. I also hope to demonstrate later that we have fallen woefully short of developing our own perspective on China, despite the high quality of research done in India on those specific areas that we have chosen to focus on. We need to be liberated from outside perspectives so that alien logic and alien agenda do not infiltrate our thinking and usurp our interests. I see the current effort as a modest contribution in that direction.

In India, we have a new generation of internationally minded youth growing up and working in environments that are influenced by global events and trends. What happens in the world matters to them in a way that cannot be grasped by their elders because those developments affect the way they live and work in our country or wherever they may go to earn a living. It is an inescapable necessity for them to have access to and knowledge of international relations as part of their working environment also for them to make informed inputs in debates about our relations with other countries and choices that we make in the development of such relations. China has forever been a great country; it was, it is and it will be a major force that has to be understood well by the broadest public of our country. It is, therefore, natural for us to develop our own perspective on China well beyond the usual comments on China's GNP and our border with them and have a broader debate beyond the arcane concerns of official diplomacy and the almost opaque public presentations emanating from official quarters on diplomatic exchanges with China.

India and China: Parallels and Comparisons

Recent times have seen a lot of pairing of India and China as well as clubbing of the two countries with two or three others, especially in the economic context. There was a short-lived Chindia (but not an Indna!), which sank rather rapidly without trace, but the BRICS, in some variations, lives on. All these are Western constructs and are obviously thought up with their parochial interests in mind. BRICS is an unprecedented beast because, unlike groupings of countries that are usually voluntary associations put together on their own volition on a perception of common interests and goals; it was thought up by a Western financial firm of controversial reputation and thrust into our consciousness without our consent or approval and without our being present at the creation. It is strange that the countries so designated have obligingly accepted the conjunction of interest as defined by someone else and spend time in summits. As the BRICS has assumed a life of its own, we will leave them aside and move on.

Let us rather look at some relevant and germane facts. 1) India and China are the two largest reservoirs of humanity in the entire world and have been so for all the time that civilisations had been created and nurtured in the world; 2) these two countries have longer histories, and more or less unbroken histories too, as unique cultures with distinctive characteristics; 3) for most of the history of civilisations, governments in these two countries, or at least in their largest portions, have ruled over larger number of people than any other ruling entity anywhere else at any time. In short, in the larger schemes of things, China and India have to measure themselves against the other and none else. There is a fourth, a more dynamic problematic fact, that the two countries began close involvement with each other on a constant basis for the first time in history only in the middle of the twentieth century.

When were We Neighbours?

This has become a far more relevant fact as the two countries embarked on their journeys as modern states at approximately the same time; India when Nehru declared on the eve of our independence that "at the stroke of midnight hour .... India will awake to life and freedom" and China a little more than two years later, when Mao Zedong stood on the ramparts of the Tiananmen in Beijing on October 1, 1949 to proclaim that "the Chinese people have now stood up". Nehru's eloquent and moving description of the moment as "something that comes, but rarely in history, when we step out from the old to the new, when an age ends, and when the soul of a nation, long suppressed, finds utterance" could equally well apply to liberated China. After much chequered endeavours and many a setbacks, both the countries had begun riding the track of rapid economic development as the fastest growing national economies. By development, one does not think solely of percentage of annual growth of GNP, but is also concerned with success in making the benefits of health, education and welfare reach the broadest mass of population, and their enjoyment of freedom based on the principles of equality, liberty and justice.

At the same time, for most of recorded history, we were strangers to each other. Much has been said about our two thousand years old friendship that is a lot of mushy nonsense. China was far away for most of our history. How many references to China do we find in our ancient literature? Kalidasa refers to 'chinamshuka', silk obviously, of the flag in the king's chariot and there is a reference in the *Mahabharata* to a 'cheena' tribe as participants in the battle. That may just be about it. The story of Ganga descending from the skies to redeem Bhagiratha's ancestors tells us the intriguing tale of the heavenly river landing on Shiva's head, an obvious reference to Mount Kailash, and flowing as seven rivers, three westward, three eastward and one, our Ganga, flowing south as the seventh branch of the sacred heavenly river. What are the three east-flowing streams? Did one or more of them flow through China? We do not know, though Ganga itself entered Chinese vocabulary in due course in the beautiful transliteration of 'heng he' (हङ् हे) or 'eternal river'. Leaving aside Chinese artifacts, which reached our peninsular region at a later time, and trade through the sea route, there does not seem to be much trade and, even more important, any significant exchange of ideas. Buddhism is a glorious exception, which we will discuss later. Outside of this specific theme and art inspired by Indian models in painting and sculpture (that too by a relatively small community, mostly outside the intellectual and cultural mainstream of China), there is absolutely nothing about India that appears to have interested the Chinese thinkers or artists.

This is so even in the modern times. Mao, who shaped modern China more than any other individual, and whose writings have influenced many outside his country including India, does not make a single reference to India in his voluminous writings. He does refer, though, to the Buddha, but in the class war context, in his famous quotation, 'we cannot expect the reactionaries to lay down their knives and become Buddha'. These are rather poor pickings for two countries, which are supposed to have been neighbours and friends for millennia, two great civilisations that have contributed so much to humanity. The rhetoric about two thousand years of friendship is a lot of froth.

The inescapable fact is that we became genuine neighbours only in the modern times, in the 20th century, when China managed to firmly rule Tibet and, thus, bring China to abut India. Like the Indian plate grinding against the Asian plate and setting up quakes, tremors and landslides, these two large masses of humanity, freighted with their own specific loads of history, are at last touching each other. What tremors are we to expect? Will they settle down and not imitate the awesome effects of plate tectonics? We do not know, for the simple reason that no two nations of comparable size, very individual histories and cultures with very little that was given to or received from the other, and with immense expectations about their own future place in the sun, have lived next to each other in human history.

That precisely is why the lessons learnt, conclusions drawn, and strategies fashioned in other cultures and societies are going to be of little use to us in studying China and working together with that country. We have to fashion our own perspective.

A Personal Aside

A brief aside about how this writer came to be interested in China, before we plunge into that fascinating country. As with many things in life, it was an accident. I joined our diplomatic service in 1965. Soon after one joins the service, one is assigned a 'compulsory foreign language', a language in which one has to achieve a certain level of proficiency before one gets the first promotion. The officer responsible for allocating languages asked which Asian language I would opt for and gave me the choice of Chinese, Japanese and Arabic. I still don't know why I said, "In that case, Chinese," but that is what I said. So it was Chinese and I went to Hong Kong in 1966 to study Chinese and onwards to Beijing in 1968 to work in our embassy during the topsy turvy days of the Cultural Revolution. It was no time to learn about China's culture or history as museums and monuments were closed; officials of our embassy could not travel outside Beijing; movie theatres did not function, traditional opera and other arts were not performed; and hardly any book other than Mao's writings was available in shops. Yet, China stays with one; one can leave China, but China does not leave one.

I never went back to China to work; therefore, the two years I spent in the university in Hong Kong learning the language did not result in optimum use for the government that paid for it. I did learn it well, though. I am also happy in retrospect that I chose Chinese rather than the other two options of Arabic and Japanese, not because they would have been inferior choices by any standard (I have worked both in Japan and Morocco, an important Arab country, with much greater experience of professional fulfilment than during my one assignment in China), but for the narrower reason of having had the opportunity to study the language well. In those days, most of the officers learning foreign languages were offered only a certain number of hours of learning, hardly sufficient to acquire fluency. Only those learning Chinese got the real immersion treatment with full time university course, examinations at regular intervals and the works.

I never went back to work in China; nor did I become an ambassador there, for some strange reason a necessary criterion for acceptance as an expert in the Indian scheme of things. I did not even get a chance to be the head of the department in the foreign office dealing with China, which also, in our scheme of things, would have qualified me as an expert even if I was innocent of the language of the region it dealt with and had never been posted there. Let that be. However, expertise has many shapes. Fluency in language is not a guarantee of expertise when it comes to China. I know the most fluent speaker of Chinese making horrendously wrong calls and persons innocent of the language providing brilliant insights.

A brief throwback to illustrate the time when I began my journey. A little after I was allotted the language, I went home and told my father, an educationist, that I was to learn Chinese. I suppose, I sounded a bit dispirited. He said, "Don't worry, it is all for the good, and there are three reasons why it is good; one, China is the biggest country and its language is the one spoken by the largest number of people as mother tongue; two, it has a great literature developed over so many centuries; and, three, it is the language of our enemy and we should learn their language so that we can understand them better." Not a very friendly sentiment, perhaps, but understandable as it was expressed four years after the border battles and one still widely prevalent in our country and something not easily wished away by the protocol platitudes or misty statements about the Asian century that is common to us.

With these introductory explanations, let us plunge into this fascinating country and find out, first, who are the Chinese.

Chapter I

China and the Chinese: Their Origins

We could say that the Chinese were always there in China and did not get there from anywhere else, at least, by the time they developed their civilisation several thousand years back in the flat plains of the Yellow River in what is northern China today. The most interesting thing about this location is that it is far away from all the other parts of the world, where what is called civilisation developed, based on agriculture, settled population, organised governments with record keeping, taxation and a military machinery that was used to protect from attack by outsiders or to control the people within. Further, the Chinese civilisation grew and reached full bloom without contacts and exchanges with other similar entities. On the other hand, the Egyptians, Greeks, the people of the Indus valley and Mesopotamia knew something, at least, about some other cultures, influenced others and were influenced by them. But China was different. In the description of Amaury de Riencourt, "Far away from the other great centres of human population, beyond the highest and bulkiest mountains of the world, beyond eternal snows, steaming jungles, inaccessible swamps and parched deserts, China was essentially a self-enclosed area – an isolated sub-continent at the far end of the known world beyond whose shores, there was nothing but an infinitely vast ocean, leading nowhere, fading away into the boundless space."[2]

Only the cultures of Central and South Americas, like the Aztec, Maya and Inca grew in comparable isolation. However, they were wiped out for all practical purposes by the Westerners who discovered them. China sustained itself as a distinct entity and a very different one from all others right into the 20th century.

For others, who came in contact with them, somewhat sporadically and in a limited way, it was very far away, the end of the known world, especially for the Europeans, as illustrated by the phrase 'from Cathay to Peru', from one extremity of the world to the other, not only by geography, but by psychological remoteness. The geographic nomenclature of 'Far East', which also suggests the same idea of remoteness, survived into the second half of the 20th century as in the UN Economic Commission of Asia and the Far East, the previous designation of the Economic and Social Commission for Asia and the Pacific. One result was that China was never colonised, no alien faith ever conquered that country, and its ethnic composition was never altered significantly through substantial mixing of races. China was always China.

A Unique Autonomous Civilisation

Of course, being far away or nearby is a matter of perspective. The Chinese naturally did not feel that way about themselves. They did not feel that they were at the end of the world, but were certain that their country was right at the centre. It was a closed world where the only other inhabitants were a few nomadic bands, all of whom were designated as 'barbarians' and given different names depending upon whether they were amenable to being civilised or not. These bands periodically burst into the Chinese space only to get absorbed and 'civilised' by China. It followed logically that they called the area they inhabited the 'Zhong Yuan' (चुङ्युआन) or 'middle plains', which eventually became 'Zhongguo', (चुङ को) the 'Middle Country', still the name for China in the Chinese language.

Thus, in the unusual environment in which they found themselves, the Chinese created a civilisation that owed very little to anyone else. Their agriculture and irrigation technologies, the art of smelting to make bronze figurines, the advanced pottery technique, all appear to be indigenously created. Even more important, their writing system too, uniquely characteristic of China, was almost certainly homegrown.[3] We will discuss later how this curious system had an equally unique impact on the Chinese character, governing system and worldview.

Gods and Kings in India and China

The Chinese of old days believed that they were ruled successively, at the earliest times, by the ancestor of all the rulers, Huang Ti, who was probably a local god, Fu Xi, who drew the magical eight sided diagram from which descended all writing; Nung, who invented agriculture; Yao and Shun, who were the perfect rulers; and, finally, Yu, who was the god who raised the Earth above water and was credited later to be the founder of the Xia dynasty. All of them were obviously mythical figures and probably local deities, but it is interesting that deities were converted into historical figures in China. One does not wish to get into specific comparisons, especially involving the perilous field of Indian history and legends, but we could still see a parallel and a contrast. Both of us believed in a past that was perfect when ideal rulers governed justly – an era from which there has been a falloff. However, the Chinese appear to have transformed the gods into ancestors and rulers, while the Indians, most probably, transformed ancestors and kings into gods. From this comes a basic divergence in the way the two civilisations viewed their past.

The First Unification and its Breakup

What we know with reasonable certainty is that in the Yellow River valley, in what is now the province of Henan (हेनान) in the geographical heart of China, various feudal states finally emerged eventually merging into the kingdom of Zhou (चौ), the first dynasty we know with certainty as having ruled a united Chinese territory. The earlier Shang (षाङ) culture, perhaps a group of feudal units with a suzerain, described as 'both barbaric and brilliant', is known to us from their elaborate tombs where people were buried to accompany the ruler in afterlife as in the Egyptian pyramids, it's beautiful bronze artifacts used primarily for religious rituals and carved jade, another important skill developed in China. The Shang people also domesticated the silkworm and created the Chinese monopoly over silk that lasted for more than 25 centuries. Thus, elements of Chinese art, like silk weaving, jade carving and casting bronze go back to truly ancient times.

Zhou, the first dynasty about which we have historical evidence, was established about 3200 years back. It absorbed the various feudal units and made what was China into a united country that was governed as a more or less centrally controlled entity. Secondly, the Zhou era saw the gradual disappearance of old religious rituals and loss of faith based on these rituals. All readers would be able to recall examples of such changes in every society and that, when such a vacuum of faith occurs, a new system of faith is created through the leadership provided by a thinker or a visionary prophet. However, what happened in China was different, perhaps unique.

Religion, in the sense of thinking about the meaning of life, an individual human being's communion with what is beyond this world, the theme of metaphysics that engaged India, West Asia and the areas of Europe influenced by the monotheistic faiths originating from West Asia just did not emerge in China. When Zhou weakened and collapsed into the era of the 'Warring States', which kept up a state of perpetual conflict and led to extensive human misery, the Chinese thought was unified, not by a prophet or a visionary seer, but by Confucius, who put together a system which was based exclusively on the precepts of ethics and a rigid hierarchy of social relations from where all otherworldly considerations were carefully purged. A third consequence flowed out of the second. It was that unity and stability of the country guaranteed by a government motivated and guided by these ethical principles became the absolutely overriding consideration of Chinese thinkers and statesmen. It followed that a united central government covering what was considered to be the territory of China was a cherished political objective and as and when the country broke up into small units, there was a great centripetal urge to put it together again in a single administrative entity. The fourth consequence of the system of Confucius and the unitary central government it espoused was the creation of a bureaucracy which was loyal to the ruler than to some abstract principles of administration. Such a bureaucracy will naturally be conservative in outlook and is meant to protect the ruler because protecting the ruler also meant, reciprocally, the protection of the interests of the bureaucracy. Such a system is simply impossible to change. The social construct created by Confucius and adopted by the country over centuries and millennia became a force for status quo. However, changes come about in any society as economic equations and productive relations change. How are the necessary changes to be brought about when the rigid system of Confucius enforced obedience to the state, the ruler, the parent and the teacher? It was here that a brilliant way out, a plan of action to alter the dead status quo, was found by Mencius, a later philosopher of the same tradition, who was honoured in China as the Second Sage. We will examine these points one by one in some detail so that we understand clearly how China has been and is governed; why China alternates between violent upheavals and a kind of stability that ends in the deadening embrace of an enervating orthodoxy.

The Zhou culture and the era troubles that followed its political demise brought forth a set of concepts and patterns of behaviour, which became ingrained in China and distinguished it for almost all time to come. The period of the 'Warring States' was brought to an end when the Qin (छिन) of north-western China conquered the whole country and unified it to impose the kind of government that has obtained in China for a very long time. The Qins were a half civilised border tribe. It is usually the half-civilised, but highly militarised groups, who are successful in unifying the area of a civilisation and providing it with an empire. The Macedonians rather than Athens unified the Greek world. The Romans rather than the Greeks unified the European classical world. Prussians known only for their military muscle unified Germany. So it goes. However, Qin ruled only from 221 to 201 BCE. The emperor called himself Shi Huang Di (षेहवाङ ती), usually translated as 'The First Emperor, but Shi means 'to begin' a sign that he intended to abolish the past, including the entire corpus of teachings of Confucius and all other theoretical writings. He failed in that attempt. The succeeding dynasty called Han (हान) established a new pattern of an alliance of imperial dictatorship based on military power in the style of the First Emperor with an administrative system founded theoretically on the principles taught by Confucius. The coalition of absolute imperial power exercised through an obedient, but ideologically motivated bureaucracy has also endured in China forever.

Chapter II

Confucius: The Founder of an Ethical System and a Philosophy of Government

Confucius is perhaps the best known Chinese in all history. His name was latinised by admiring western scholars of the 17th and 18th centuries to confer on him a rank and honour similar to that enjoyed by great thinkers of their society. It was this admiration following the introduction of his thought in the West, originally by the Jesuit missionaries, who travelled to and lived in China in the 17th century, that elevated Confucius to the status of a sage whose teachings were of universal significance. It also created the image of China, which was supposedly governed all the time by the enlightened precepts of such a wise man as a perfect and harmonious society where everybody lived happily in perfect attunement with nature, a country at the very acme of refinement, of the most elegant and gracious culture. Therefore, it was the image of Confucius rather than what he actually said or did that happened to become far more meaningful and effective in the wider world, especially because it was a remarkable exception to the belief of the Westerners from that era onwards that Western thought set the norm and established the agenda for all humanity.

Confucius is the latinised version of Kung Fu Zi (खुङ फूसे) or The Great Master Kung. Kung was his surname. He is believed to have been born in 551 BCE in the state of Lu, which is approximately identical to the modern province of Shandong (षानतुङ) in eastern China. It was a time when the China of the Zhou dynasty had broken up into many units ruled by powerful nobles constantly at war with one another and oppressing their people with forced labour and heavy taxes. Naturally, the era was designated by later historians as the 'era of the warring states'. Although Confucius was acknowledged as one of the wisest men of his times, his wish to be the advisor to his ruler so that he could put his ideas into practice mostly came to naught. Therefore, he took to teaching and training younger men in the hope that they, at least, would assume positions of authority and implement his ideas. He did get some positions in later years, but he moved from area to area, to finally come home where he died in 479 BCE.

The three great ancient societies of India, China and Greece produced three wise men, the Buddha, Confucius and Socrates, at approximately the same time, when all the three societies were facing similar challenges of collapse of traditional faiths, questioning of traditional rituals, division of the society into warring states and the resultant political instability and internecine wars. All of them are known for their wisdom imparted through their lectures and conversation, which were reduced to writing by faithful disciples. Confucius was mostly ignored by his contemporaries, the Shakyamuni was honoured by the rulers of his generation, and Socrates was denounced for his alleged crimes of atheism and corrupting the young and put to death. All of them spoke the language of rationality and refused to speak of the world beyond the human ken. It would be interesting to compare and contrast the three thinkers and the societies that produced them in fairly similar stages of political and social disintegration and try to account for their differing experiences, the different impacts they had on their contemporaries. However, here we will limit ourselves to presenting some of the thoughts of the Chinese sage, how they evolved under later thinkers, and how they influenced China over a very long period of time. Readers can draw their own conclusions about the three sages and their very different impacts on their own societies and the world at large.

His Basic Teachings

Thirteen texts are accepted as constituting the canon of classical Confucian texts, though not all of them have to do specifically with the Master per se. They deal with a variety of subject matters including poetry, divination, historical records, rules of rituals, and sources of the teachings of the Master. Even the latter are not the writings of Confucius, but compilations based on his teachings. One great classic in the collection is the work of Mencius or Meng Zi (मङ्ड से), Master Meng, who lived between 371 and 289 BCE, a text that was included to the original canon in the 12th century.

The first thing to know about Confucius is that he was not a religious teacher. He talked about Heaven, but as an abstract thing without any suggestion of the supernatural. He had no interest in metaphysics. He founded Chinese philosophy and turned it away permanently from metaphysics and all related themes. He talked about humanity, ethics and relations among humans.

He said, "Virtue is to love men. Wisdom is to understand men." This principle is summarised in the idea of 'ren' (.षन). Like our dharma, it is a very difficult word and concept to render in one word or phrase in another language as it constitutes a set of ethos. A commentary from very old days explained that 'ren is to love men joyously and from the innermost of one's heart'. There is no material reward in living a life of 'ren', but one will 'not seek to live at the expense of injuring their ren and will even sacrifice their lives to preserve their ren intact.' One natural expression of 'ren' that is manifested from early life is filial piety, a virtue that was extolled beyond all others by later commentators and extended to include loyalty to the ruler from the ruled.

This principle was fully developed by Mencius, who proposed that four virtues – compassion, modesty, sense of shame and distinction between right and wrong – were universal in mankind, and were expressions of the four virtues of ren, decorum, righteousness and wisdom. Education was to be aimed at cultivating these qualities. On the other hand, evil was the neglect of these qualities. Human nature was innately good when guided by these feelings, like water flowing naturally downwards. Mencius famously illustrated this by giving the example of a person instinctively rushing to save a child ignoring danger to oneself.

Qualifications for a Ruler

A person who has cultivated virtue would be superior – he is 'concerned with virtue, an inferior man is concerned with land' or 'the superior man understands what is right; an inferior man understands what is profitable' as taught by Confucius. The other side of the argument is that the superior man was the one, who had the right to rule because of the moral qualities that earned him the leadership position. This was not anti-democratic in theory because anyone willing to cultivate himself could aspire to that position. In fact, it denied the right of an elite to rule by the right of being an elite by birth and was, thus, profoundly different from all other ancient theories of governance.

Therefore, it was the personal character and conduct of the ruler that was the central and critical factor in good governance. He has to set an example. Confucius taught, "To govern is to set things right. If you begin by setting yourself right, who will deviate from the right?" Such a ruler is obviously good and his rule benign. It follows that such a ruler is to be respected and obeyed unreservedly. Through such logic, the principle of loyalty towards one's parents was extended by Confucius to the ruler too. When the ruler is seen as a model and demands the same degree of respect as one's parents, it becomes a recipe of unquestioning obedience and docile imitation. When a ruler is benign, competent and powerful, he inspires his people, their energies are rightly channelised, the country flourishes; by the same token, a weak or corrupt ruler brings the entire country to its knees, leading to chaos and anarchy. Conquering and ruling a country as vast as China requires phenomenal leadership qualities. It is true that most of the founders of dynasties were real geniuses, charismatic leaders of men, capable administrators and brilliant military commanders. Every dynasty has a superb beginning. However, dynastic succession also meant that all kinds of men succeeded the founder. Bad rulers caused disaffection, but the Confucian dicta enjoined obedience even to such rulers. The removal of such a ruler created a dilemma in the light of the incontrovertible principle of loyalty. China had to wait till Mencius found a brilliant solution to this problem, a solution that had a lasting impact on how China is governed.

How to Remove a Ruler and Still Be a Loyal Subject

Mencius reaffirmed Confucius's thought that the government has to exist and work for the good of the people. He also affirmed the Master's teaching that people have the obligation to obey the ruler. Confucius had said, "Let the prince be prince, minister be minister, the father the father and the son the son". The question is the right course of action when the ruler does not uphold the virtue of 'ren' and fails in his duty. It was to solve this problem within the scope of Confucian thought that Mencius conceived the idea of 'mandate from Heaven', the concept that authority is naturally conferred on the ruler because of his virtue and abilities. By the same logic, the absence of such virtues and abilities was to be deemed the withdrawal of the mandate and the removal of the authority to govern. The right may be divine, but it is never unconditional or open ended. A tyrannical government, by its nature, is without mandate from Heaven and it is justified to remove such a ruler. Obviously, there is an unavoidable element of *a priori* judgment in this theory, but it was a practical solution to a grave problem. Mencius was asked how the assassination of Zhou Wang was justified when loyalty to the ruler was the basic duty of all subjects, and he made the memorable response, "I have heard that a despicable creature called Zhou was put to death, but I have not heard anything about a murder of a sovereign." A bad ruler is no ruler at all by the fact of his being bad and should indeed be overthrown. To rebel in such situations was not only justified, but was surely one's duty.

This ruling from one of the most honoured teachers had an enormous impact on Chinese political practice for all time to come. On the one side, loyalty made for a rigid and inflexible political system. On the other, the only permitted way of removing a ruler was rebellion. How is one to know whether the 'mandate from heaven' is withdrawn? By trying to overthrow the ruler. Increasing misery of ordinary people, whether from misrule, lawlessness or natural calamities were all seen as signs of the withdrawal of the mandate and an invitation to armed rebellion. If the rebellion was successful, it was proof that the government that was overthrown was indeed evil. Thus, every dynasty invited rebellion at the first sign of weakness and failure on the expectation that it would be legitimised ex post facto by a successful outcome. The eventually successful rebel assumed the throne as the recipient of the fresh mandate from Heaven. Thus, the Qin, who unified China first, was overthrown by Liu Bang (ल्यू पाङ), who established the Han dynasty, which gave the Chinese people their ethnic identity.

It's Relevance to Today's China

This is no old story from ancient history. Mao, the Marxist revolutionary, said during his armed campaign against the Guomindang (कोमिनताङ) that what he had learned from Marx was that 'to rebel was justified', a teaching of Mencius rather than Marx. It was not that strange either that Mao said so because he was deeply versed in Chinese classics and was inspired by their examples. At the same time, the Chairman, who being unfamiliar with any foreign language could not have studied Marx in similar detail because the full translation of *Das Kapital* was published only in 1939 much after Mao established full control over the Chinese Communist Party and had composed many of his path-breaking theoretical essays which were acknowledged as original contributions to the communist thought. Mao never forgot the thought and teaching of the Second Sage. When he launched the Cultural Revolution in 1966 to fight his inner Party enemies, Mao wrote a wall poster for his followers as the first salvo in the battle, 'zaofan youli' – to rebel is justified – a phrase that became the motto and the slogan for Red Guards as they attacked the Party and government officials throughout the country!

The other side of the coin is that Chinese rulers had to be sensitive to any sign of public distemper. There is no way they can say that they have a mandate for a fixed term like the life of a Parliament that they are determined to hold on to, while hoping that something will turn up and save them at the next election. Famine, floods, draught, eruption of locusts, anything that disrupted the balance of nature in an agricultural society was obviously a sign of the displeasure of Heaven, a warning about the possible withdrawal of the mandate to govern, not something to be ignored as vagaries of nature or immutable fate beyond man's control as other societies are wont to do. Even a natural disaster that cannot be controlled by earthly rulers could be seen as a sign. This belief too survives to this day. A terrible earthquake flattened the mining town of Tangshan in 1976, killing a quarter of a million people. For the ordinary Chinese, it was a sure sign of a change in the mandate, the impending death of a great leader. The passing away of Chairman Mao within three months, an obviously unconnected event, would have appeared to them as validating the ancient belief.

The system devised by Confucius and retained by the Chinese empire till early 20th century was deemed to be the perfect governing system fit for the grandest of states. Therefore, when China was attacked and defeated by the Western countries, and later by Japan, it created not just a political and military shock, but a profound collapse of faith in the system that has remained unchanged for more than 2000 years. When scholars started thinking how to save their country from being broken up or colonised, all of them identified the Confucian system as the primary weakness of China, the biggest obstacle to progress and modernity. Elimination of the influence of Confucius was the prime objective of all modernizing forces, especially the Communist Party.

It is all the more ironic that the government run by the same Communist Party has named the institutes established abroad for the promotion of Chinese culture after the once reviled Confucius.

Chapter III

Creation and Growth of the Chinese Empire

The Zhou unification laid the foundation for the unification of China and the concept of an emperor who ruled the entire Chinese universe. The horrors of the period of the warring states only proved the validity of this concept because the absence of a united government caused much misery to the people. During this period, the Chinese started to spread their settlements beyond the Yellow River valley. Being cultivators, they moved southward to the Yangzi (याङ से) valley and beyond, reclaiming land, mixing with the communities already living there, and gradually making them Chinese in language and habits. New kingdoms were established in the regions south of the Yangzi of which some like Chu (क्षू) were powerful as well as centres of culture. Liu Bang, the founder of the Han dynasty, who overthrew the Qin and created the first all-China dynasty was actually from Chu. The Chinese never tried to settle in the steppes of the north, always retaining the distinction between the steppe and the sown. However, the people in the south, who spoke different languages or dialects, were not quite dissimilar and could be absorbed and made into Chinese. The southerners also accepted this change with hardly any resistance unlike the nomads of the steppe. China, the state, thus spread to the very limits of China, the continent, establishing a repeatedly demonstrated political and emotional compulsion for the state to fill the geographical spread of the continent. The existence of many states within that sphere was deemed an aberration, an unnatural state of affairs requiring correction even when it existed for decades or centuries. The creation of a centrally administered state that controlled a very large area also produced, inevitably and necessarily, a heavily governed state, a hard state, quite the opposite of another piece of advice from the Second Master, Mencius, "A state should be governed like cooking a small fish – very little."

In this matter too, readers can mull over the difference with India where the emperor, who brought the entire sub-continent under one umbrella was a theoretical concept hardly ever realized in practice, a country that has maintained willy nilly a multi-state system with logical consequences of varying habits of people, uneven quality of governance and administrative conduct in different areas, multiplicity of languages, inescapable demands of federalism and respect for multiple identities, not to mention the existence of several sovereign states within one geographic, and may we say the same cultural and strategic, space in uneasy balance at the best and outright hostility at the worst.

As they spread southward, the Chinese took the strategic decision not to expand their regime and zone of culture in the direction of north and absorb the nomad, considering it profitless to conquer their country. On the other hand, they also decided to ensure that the dangerous barbarian was prevented from intruding into China. However, they did enter China repeatedly, only to be absorbed in their turn and become Chinese. Different kingdoms built small walls both to stop the barbarians and to prevent their people from getting out. The irony is that the Qins, who conquered China, were themselves semi-barbarians from the northern edges of China. The Great Wall is associated with Qin Shi Huang Di, who linked many existing walls and extended the whole thing using forced labour. The Wall was primarily a defensive structure and this objective becomes clear when we note that it is neither 'great' nor 'wall' in the Chinese language but is, in fact, Changcheng, which translates as 'long fort'.

Myths about the Great Wall

There are many myths about the Great Wall and its present situation is overly hyped. One of them is that it is the only human construction that can be seen from the Moon. This is nonsense because even large natural features of the earth cannot be seen from our satellite (Armstrong mistook a cloud formation for the Wall and the first Chinese astronaut acknowledged that he could not see anything like the Wall). Yet this canard is much repeated including ad nauseam during the Beijing Olympics. Most of the wall is in ruins and only a small portion of what was built survives. Another myth is that the Qin emperor had the whole original wall built. Actually, the portion tourists go to see near Beijing was constructed during the late days of the Ming dynasty about 500 years back, making it pretty recent among great monuments. The place tourists drive to from Beijing for a look at the Great Wall is actually a reconstruction by the Communist government that was opened only on March 19, 1960.[4]

It was also a somewhat pointless structure because it repeatedly and consistently failed to do the assigned job of defending China. There were many invasions across it and two major successes in breaching it by the Mongols and the Manchus, who conquered and ruled China, respectively, as the Yuan and Qing (छिङ) dynasties. For such a failure, it cost an inordinate amount of money and lives. A folk song from the Qin times lamented that the Wall was 'propped up on human skeletons'. The cost of the Wall was one of the causes of the collapse of the Ming dynasty.

As with Confucius, the image of the Wall was also manufactured in the West, once again, starting with the Jesuits, who lived in China. The 'long fort' became the 'Great Wall' and it was just another step to aver that the people, who built something that 'great' were surely 'great', as Nixon finally made explicit in his arrival statement in Beijing in 1972. This suits the present day Chinese fine as they put the name in everything from matchboxes to luxury hotels, because it is a rare usable item from the wreckage of China's past, most of which had been rejected by the communists as feudal and exploitative. The structure that was once reviled as the symbol of oppression is now the sign of China's greatness, just as Confucius, who once stood for all that was regressive in China, is now the icon of Chinese civilisation.

Unity of China: A Unique Phenomenon among States

The unity of China and its repeated unification after each breakup is a unique phenomenon among large countries. It is something of a truism of geo-politics that countries that spread north-south have a harder time remaining under a united government than those that stretch east-west. The spread across latitudes produces significant differences in climate, leading to different agricultural practices, styles of living and temperaments. 'Annadbhavati bhutani', says the Gita wisely. Even relatively small countries like Britain and Italy that are stretched north-south are no exception to this general principle as is seen in the difference between the Scot and the English or between the Milanese and the Neapolitan. As our history shows, empires based in the north Indian plains not only ran into difficulties, but even faced the threat of collapse every time they made the fateful decision to cross the Vindhyas in a drive for expansion. Further, unlike Italy and Britain, where mountains lie along the country, India has a major mountain barrier across the country. Geography is not the only problem. Even the USA, a state created by an ideology rather than geographical factors alone, had well known problems in remaining united. The two regions of the USA have always remained divided politically and the South has its distinct personality as it does in India too.

In the case of China, north-south differences do exist and there have been regional prejudices, but being Chinese overrode such considerations, at least, among the educated and the elite. There are several reasons for this. Most important, people of the north migrated to south and were large enough in number to have absorbed the local population to create a homogenous mix. The hills of China were not forbidding barriers like the Vindhyas. There are other causes unique to China, like the Confucian ideology, which eliminated local aberrations in favour of a standard product. The second element is the written language with ideograph characters, which ensured that dialectal variations did not lead to different written languages and break the country up, as happened in Europe after Latin evolved into different languages and many languages of India were born from Sanskrit. We will return to this in detail later.

The Importance of History in China

It is necessary to spend some time not only on the facts of Chinese history, but also on why history is so important for us to know China better. Primarily, it is important because the Chinese consider it important, they talk about it, refer to it for precedents, and use events of the past as allegories for current political and economic debates. Only in China would one have to read ancient history to unravel the current political quarrels. The Cultural Revolution started with a denunciation in 1965 of a play, *The Dismissal of Hai Rui,* which dealt with the tribulations of an honest high official, who lived a thousand years back. One had to learn the history of the Song dynasty and draw parallels between the historical personalities and contemporary leaders to decode the signals that the play conveyed about inner Party conflicts to understand that the play was a veiled attack on Mao's policies during the late 1950s and the punishment meted out by him to Marshal Peng Dehuai, who commanded the Chinese troops in the Korean war. The Chinese quote history; we, in India, quote epics.

By the time Confucius started to put together his ideas in an integrated system, the Chinese had more or less given up their traditional beliefs and methods of worship, which lasted for more than a thousand years. Their mythology faded away and died. Rituals were replaced by worship of ancestors. Even those rites were seen by scholars as purely symbolic with no spiritual content. The peasant, on the other hand, has his superstitions and a dash of Buddhism to keep his spirits alive. We have already seen the way the Chinese transformed the gods of the old days into ancestors, who, they asserted, actually lived once upon a time and were thus eligible to be worshipped. To worship the ancestors, one has to remember them, record them in annals, thus placing history on a special pedestal. In Greece, history was a grand art form with its own Muse Clio along with other arts like Tragedy, Comedy and Lyric poetry. In China, history was made to fit the official moral philosophy and, in the absence of myths and legends, historical events and personages became examples. Past was observed and studied for the sake of the present and the future.

While presenting his historical work to the emperor, Sima Qian (सेमा छ्यिन), the father of Chinese historiography, who lived in the 2nd century BCE, wrote, "Your majesty may pardon this vain attempt for the sake of his loyal intention, and in moments of leisure will deign to cast a sacred glance over this work so as to learn from the rise and fall of the previous dynasties the secret of the successes and failures of the present hour." Much later, the famous Tai Zong Emperor of the Tang dynasty wrote, "By using a mirror of brass, you may see to adjust your cap; by using antiquity as a mirror, you may learn to foresee the rise and fall of empires."[5] Thus, everything that was done by a ruler was recorded. In fact, one of the Classics associated with Confucius is a somewhat dry record of the happenings of the kingdom of Lu during the time of the sage, which was used by later writers for much subtle commentaries and extraction of moral ideas through the kind of textual criticism and exegesis that was used in other societies for the study of their sacred texts.

Chinese historiography was also tied to the rise and fall of dynasties. The official histories of dynasties were written after each of them fell, after a decent interval, under the sponsorship of the next dynasty. It was a carefully doctored effort because the aim was not to research, record and analyse events and trends, but to explain how the 'mandate from Heaven' was withdrawn from the previous dynasty so that the seizure of power by the current dynasty stood justified. This process took a few decades and the result was frozen, sealed in amber. It was never an independent effort of research, but a planned attempt to arrive at predetermined conclusions. As Balasz puts it, it was the 'most massive monument ever raised to glorify a social class',[6] which never criticised the way the previous dynasty came to power. This authorized text was called 'shi ji' or authentic record and no other attempt to study the past was allowed once the sole record was compiled. It is this process carried out through out China's history under the guidelines of Confucius laid down in 5th century BCE and never amended that is extolled by others as China's great sense of history and long range vision and contrasted with a touch of condescension with what is called the absence of historic vision in India! This view, held rather widely though uncritically, which has acquired the position of conventional wisdom if not sacred text status, deserves searching examination.

History in India and China

As seen from the views of the founder of Chinese historiography and a great emperor quoted above, history was seen in China as a guide for future and not as an analysis of the past. In other words, it had a moral role through offering examples, both positive and negative. History in China took the place of moral codes that arose from religion in other societies to fill the vacuum left by the elimination of religion from the central position it enjoyed elsewhere. Therefore, it cannot be true that the high status given to history in China is an indication of China's long term perspective etc. Their aim was only to write the definitive history of the previous dynasty on the basis of accepted Confucian principles. Once written down, it was never allowed to be revised or reassessed on the basis of new research or evidence. It is not acceptable that the recording of the doings of dynasty after dynasty by the next one in an officially sanctioned political exercise is elevated to long term perspective about the future. There is no logical connection between the two. There is no logic to the argument that careful recording of the past is evidence for long term view of future.

Nor can we so arbitrarily condemn India as without a sense of history. A society which claims to fix the start of the Kali era exactly was certainly capable of counting years and months and days. The optical illusion here is that the Chinese history was about the whole of China and there is nothing parallel in India with a similar centralised perspective. That is why Amaury de Riencourt, who wrote books on the 'souls' of China and India, says that China was a historian's paradise, but something similar happened in India only after the advent of Islam here.[7] He evidently neglected to note that India, thanks to its more open geographical location and physical features, was neither a centrally administered political entity nor thought of itself as the Middle Kingdom with none but barbarian tribes abutting it. It was an area with vast contacts all around with exchange of goods and ideas on an uninterrupted basis. The centralised perspective he speaks of developed quite naturally with the court historians of the Sultans and the Padishahs, several of whom styled themselves as the 'ruler of the world' and concerned themselves primarily with recording their activities – not substantially different from that of the court historian of China working for the universal emperor – a circumstance that would not have appealed to the writers in the earlier multi-state system within the Indian civilisational space, who accepted that there was a world out there beyond theirs – nor, for that matter, those living in the parts of India outside the jurisdiction of those 'rulers of the world', who wrote their own history from their individual perspectives, no matter whether it was considered parochial or not; therefore, such a centralised conceptualisation and narrative was neither desirable nor viable.

Chinese historiography was always that of the dynasty and served state interests. It did not provide for any narrative other than that of the dynasty and by the dynasty. On the other hand, the Indian multi-state system allowed telling of stories from the various regional points of view in their own languages. Once written down, the Chinese narratives were neither challenged nor amended. There was no scope for the people without access to the written word to tell the story. In India, those without access to the written word could realise their own version of history through folklores, legends, stories of local heroes and tales of individual communities. All these devices of self-identification were beyond the pale in the Chinese system, which privileged the written word to the exclusion of the spoken word and the elite at the expense of the masses.

Chapter IV

The Chinese System of Government

We have found that China broke up into many small kingdoms after the collapse of the Zhou dynasty. Despite the constant warfare, it was a very dynamic time socially. Feudalism collapsed at the same time because inheritance by the eldest son fell into disuse and family land was divided up, spreading ownership rights wider. This was one of the reasons for the push of the Chinese from the Yellow River southwards, as the surplus population of a fertile community looked for new lands to settle. The oldest Chinese crop was millet followed by wheat and, in the southern regions, rice. Large scale irrigation works also became necessary with extensive cultivation of the superior grains. The next step was the building of small fortified towns, which became the administrative centres of small states. The Chinese ideograph for 'state' is guo (को), an eloquent picture of an enclosed space with the symbols of a weapon and a mouth inside. It was such a society that was brought under a single ruler by Qin Shi Huang Di, when he completed his conquests in 221 BCE.

The First Emperor, the Creator of Chinese Government

Though shortlived, the Qin established the pattern of government in China. He called himself the First Emperor because his objective was to abolish the past. The times preceding his conquest was an age of warfare, but it was also an age in which many philosophic schools also conducted battles of ideas, celebrated as the times when 'hundred flowers bloomed'. The Qin terminated all such debates and silenced the scholars. He was the original book burner in all history, because he thought that all books were useless except those dealing with agriculture and divination. When Confucian scholars protested the destruction of books, he ordered them to be buried alive. To ensure uniformity of administration over his huge domain, he standardised weights and measures and even fixed the length of axles of carts that moved goods along the roads. Most important, and quite interesting for a man who burned books, he ordered the standardisation of the writing system that enforced the uniformity of the ideographs. The Qin tax policies also encouraged the practice of land being divided among sons. This helped prevent the creation of a feudal landholding elite in China and led to the rise of a peasant class that was the tenant of the state. The elimination of the feudal phase in the social history of China also helped in the perpetuation of an authoritarian and centralized imperial rule carried out through appointed officials rather than through local chiefs.

The First Emperor also created the system of sending two persons to each locality as administrators so that they could keep a check on each other. It was not efficient, but effective for control from the centre, which was more important to the emperor than financial prudence. Such a duplication of power is also a regular characteristic of Chinese administration even today with a Party Secretary sharing power with the administrative head and the political commissar sharing authority with the commander in military units.

Finally, the emperor began building the Great Wall as a defensive measure. It was done with forced labour, killing a large number of people in a task which, in fact, failed to achieve its objective of keeping invaders out. However, the Qin Empire, put together more than two thousand years back, remained the core

China. Every time the empire disintegrated, it was put together in roughly the same shape as the Qin Empire with periodic accumulations that had come to stay till China, as we know, took shape under the Qing dynasty in the 17th century and was reconstructed in the same shape by the Communist government in the 20th century.

A quick review of the list will show how the First Emperor was instrumental in creating a social and administrative system that endured right into the 20th century. It is also true that the way states are originally put together in the first place has very important consequences for the way they are governed. The governing apparatus put together by the First Emperor and his successor of the Han dynasty is worth study because it tells us much about the way China is still governed.

Before we take leave of this remarkable man, let us also learn what happened when he died. The First Emperor was terribly afraid of death and spent a lot of time in rituals to avoid the inevitable. He was also constantly on the move, personally inspecting some part of the empire or the other. During one of these visits, he died on a hot summer day in a place far away from the capital Changan, the present day Xian (शीआन). His prime minister, who wanted to put the pliable second son of the emperor on the throne, secretly sent word to the capital in the name of the emperor commanding his elder son to commit suicide (which he obediently did), loaded the dead body of the emperor in a cart with another carrying fish right behind it to mask the odour of the dead body and eventually reached the capital to bury him in the tomb, which is now a great tourist attraction. The prime minister's favourite was put on the throne, but the dynasty vanished in the matter of a few years. What lessons were drawn by the Chinese from this story of intriguing prime ministers, who put incompetent favourites on the throne, only for the nation to come to grief.

Han dynasty: Consolidation through Marriage of Military Power and Confucian Ethics

The empire established by the First Emperor collapsed, but the system endured. China was ruled for all time to come by an authoritarian system as a unitary state with the aid of a bureaucracy that ensured uniformity of procedures within, while trying to ensure that it remained impervious to events beyond its borders. Even the declaration of the Republic in 1912 and the Peoples' Republic in 1949 have not altered matters that much. Is it not striking that official visitors are taken to visit the excavated tomb of the First Emperor and the army of soldiers, who guard him in his death sleep, but nobody is ever invited to make an official visit to the birthplace of Confucius or to pay respects at the tomb of Dr. Sun Yatsen, the moving spirit behind the overthrow of imperial rule and progress towards democracy, at Nanjing, not even to see the tiny building in Shanghai where the Chinese Communist Party was born in 1921, although Mao, the founding father of the PRC, was one of the twelve men present at that first step in the journey of ten thousand miles?

Liu Bang and the Han Dynasty

The short-lived empire of Qin was overthrown in 206 BCE by Liu Bang, who established the Han dynasty, which ruled for more than 400 years. Liu Bang conquered a larger area than Alexander, Caesar or Napoleon and created an empire far larger and far more durable than what the three men, extolled by the West as the greatest military geniuses, ever managed to put together. It is a sign of the way we learn about the world that the man whose work shaped the largest country in the world for two thousand years is unknown outside his country. The Han gave its name to the people. The Chinese are ethnic Hans. Their writing, though standardised by the Qin, is described as having Han characters. The new emperor rehabilitated the Confucian scholars and made the teachings of their Master the basis of governing China. The Han started the method of choosing officials of the government through an examination in which candidates had to write elegant essays on academic subjects. The thoughts of Master Kung became the official ideology of the state. The unchanging ideology had such an iron grip for such a long time that it became the prime object of criticism and denunciation in early 20th century, when China collapsed under alien attacks and was desperately seeking the means to save itself. At the same time, the basic system conceived and implemented by the first Han emperor, centralisation of administration, the concept that law emanates from the supreme ruler and is based on an ideology, which the entire nation subscribes to and, finally, a bureaucracy that runs the administration on the basis of its commitment to the ideology and loyalty to the individual in supreme authority, essentially endured and, in fact, became deeper rooted in the modern times.

A Quick Dash through Centuries

Thus was set the pattern of Chinese history. Time passed; dynasties decayed; rebels made their repeated attempts; and finally succeeded. The successful rebel became the new emperor; his court historians eventually recorded the final version of the history of the previous rulers, taking decades to doctor it so that it would align with already laid down theories; his officials restored the state administration that was in disarray; and the cycle resumed. The barbarians from the north were repelled or absorbed. Others from beyond the desert or the seas were welcomed and declared to be tributaries of the emperor, whose rule extended to the entire world. We have already seen how the dynasties rose and fell with successful rebellions under brilliant leaders, followed by slow decay. Han (206 BCE – 220 CE) was followed by Sui (स्वे) (581 CE – 618 CE), Tang (थाङ) (618 – 907 CE) and the Song (सुङ) (960—1126 CE). Then, the barbarians broke through to capture northern China. The Song retreated to the south and lingered on till 1279. The invading Mongols established their capital in China in 1267 in the place called Cambaluc or 'Khan's town' under Kublai Khan, who founded the Yuan dynasty. It was this town of

Cambaluc, which was renamed Beijing or Northern Capital by the first emperor of the Ming dynasty, which was in power from 1368 to 1644 CE. They were removed by another alien group, this time from Manchuria, who ruled as the Qing till the end of the imperial government in China. A revolt that started on October 10, 1911 in the city of Wuhan in Central China culminated in the declaration of a Chinese republic and the abdication of the last emperor on February 12, 1912.

This quick run through two thousand years will show that China had come under the pressure of external invasion in the 10th century, when half its territory fell under foreign control. Since then, China had rulers of alien origin for more than half the time. It also shows that China was divided into small states for nearly one-third of the time in the last two thousand years. Further, many of the rulers of these small kingdoms were of nomad origin as were the Qin and probably the Tang. China has a long history of being broken up into smaller kingdoms and successful foreign invasions. The impression that one dynasty followed the other smoothly to rule the entire nation is just a pleasant myth. At the same time, the urge to reunite the country under a strong central government never diminished as seen from the success of the fresh dynasties that rose to power and ruled all over China or, at least, almost all of it.

Expansion of China beyond the Cultivated Zone

Till the Manchurians, who ruled as Qing, came on the scene in the 17th century, China had always limited itself to regions that suited its agriculture based way of life. For the first time, the Qing moved west and filled the sparsely populated and lightly governed areas all the way to the Czar's empire, just as the Russians were exploring Central Asia and Siberia and annexing as much territory as they could to their empire. For the first time, the Chinese empire included and ruled on a regular basis, large areas of exclusively non-Chinese population, which were equal in area to the traditional Chinese territory of the Han race. The Chinese government does not like it to be so phrased and insists that all the areas were 'always Chinese', but it was, in fact, just another case of imperial expansion and conquest. Our experience of imperialism and colonialism arriving in ships should not make us forget that they could equally well arrive on foot, on horseback or with the aid of internal combustion engines. Otherwise, the Qing would not have any reason to organise the predominantly Muslim areas to the West as a new province formally named Xinjiang (शिनचियाङ) or New Borders. If it was 'always China', how come it was 'new' in 1884 when the province was so named?

Foreign Relations in the Imperial Days

In theory, the Chinese empire had nothing like foreign relations for the simple reason that they just did not conceive of the idea that there was any place on earth that was not under the sway of their emperor. There were, of course, nomadic tribes beyond the ken of the empire, mere vassals who bore periodic tributes to the ruler whose duty was to maintain peace and harmony throughout the world through his just conduct and periodic rituals to please the powers above. The Chinese hardly accepted nomads as humans and the Chinese characters for the names of these tribes and bands included symbols for insects, animals and worms. Even the Japanese and the Vietnamese were called 'mosquitoes and scorpions' by the first Ming emperor! The Great Wall had gates with names like 'Tower to Suppress the North', 'Fort that Overawes the Goat-like Barbarians' and 'Gate to Enter the Glorious Civilisation'.

However, the practical problem was that the tribes that pressed on China's north and northwest did not accept these rules and arrangements. Instead, they invaded regularly and conquered occasionally. Therefore, for most of history, China's policy for 'suppression of barbarians' was a combination of a) defensive arrangements, like the Great Wall; b) forward policy of attack and destruction that was carried out under strong emperors; and c) playing various tribes against each other, which also involved funding and financing the selected ones so that those willing to coexist with China could be used to check the others. All these have been in existence for such a long time that they can be said to be ingrained habits, reflexes that show up even in current practice as – a) prickly aggressiveness about territory and building of new Walls, like censorship of internet, etc.; b) attempt to overawe small neighbours with threats and military operations when China judged them to be necessary; and c) playing one neighbour against another to keep all of them at bay.

The other side of the belief that the emperor ruled everywhere was that there was no scope for nationalism in old China. Nationalism follows an agreement among people about somebody to unite against. Where was the enemy to unite against when the emperor ruled everybody under the sky?

Given its view of itself as the centre of culture, the Chinese empire never thought of contacts with other states as equal exchanges. This is where the concept of tribute was constructed. Chinese historians recorded in their annals that various barbarian tribes acknowledged the emperor as their suzerain and came bearing tributes. This claim has been analysed extensively by scholars, who have established that many of these so called tribute missions were actually trade negotiations. The central Asian communities brought stuff they wanted to sell and bargained for barter with Chinese goods. There have been cases where they went back without giving any 'tribute' because they could not agree on barter terms. The Chinese also had to offer goods of greater value because the emperor as the suzerain had to be generous. Thus, the tribute system was a non-military solution to the problem, but a costly proposition for China. They also had to frequently appease the nomad chiefs by even offering a Chinese princess as his consort as part of the negotiations.

A note in the Chinese annals that somebody came with tribute does make it so, as was the case with the famous British expedition of the 18th century. The Chinese had diplomatic contacts with Rome, Japan and Indian kingdoms, all of which were claimed by the Chinese to be tribute missions by vassals from faraway lands. The great emperors, Rajaraja Chola and Rajendra Chola, had sent envoys to China. They would only have been amused if they were told that they were vassals of the Chinese emperor.

A real problem arose for China when the Russians arrived in late 17th centuries at the border of Manchuria, the ancestral home of the Qing emperor. The border was demarcated for the first time and a treaty was drawn up with the assistance of the Jesuit missionaries living in Beijing. The Treaty of Nerchinsk was the first such treaty of China with another country in which China negotiated as an equal partner and acknowledged another ruler, at least implicitly, as equal to the Emperor, who claimed to rule everything under the heaven. No similar process took place with another country till the 19th century when arbitrary agreements were imposed on China through military pressure by various western countries and Japan.

A related issue is kowtow. This is an ancient Chinese ritual of respect similar to falling at the feet of elders that is practised in India. It became an issue only because the Westerners made it into an issue. The Western envoys never had any problem in kneeling before Western emperors, but they took umbrage when it came to China, which suggests a racist angle to their objection. The Chinese did not merely make demands on others because their own envoys to Russia performed the kowtow before the Czar in early 18th century. Much is made for no reason at all about the kowtow being a sign of Chinese claim to superiority, but it is no such thing.

The problem for China was that, with the exception of Russia with whom they had only sporadic dealings, they had no experience of living cheek by jowl with another properly governed country, another empire embodying a different civilisational ethos that could challenge it not just militarily, but also ideologically and culturally. The net result was that the overlapping of the ethnic, geographical, political, literary and cultural spaces created a unique self-sufficiency that made China impervious to external influences and disdainful of cultural interaction. However, what is legitimate self-confidence in one age becomes pitiable complacency in another. When such an impact was felt in the 19th century, China's limitations were pitilessly exposed. It was all the more cruel because the country that did so was Japan, a country that was long considered to have borrowed all that it had as civilisation from China. The Japanese went to war in the 1890s over Korea and defeated the Chinese so surprisingly easily as to shock both the losers and the winners. The shock was so overwhelming that China spent the next century and half struggling with it politically, culturally and emotionally. China as victim, a nation that suffered exceptional humiliation, was the end product of this demoralising experience, an emotional state that still persists and colours its dealings with others. It also followed that this situation has to be corrected, accounts settled properly, the dignity and self-respect of the nation not just restored, but it is also ensured that the restored status is acknowledged in a proper manner by all, especially those, who humiliated China in the past.

Chapter V

Art, Culture and Science in China

The Language

Modern Standard Chinese is based on the speech of Beijing. It is mistakenly called Mandarin and should properly be called the Common Speech (Putonghua) or national language (Guoyu). Mandarin is not the name of a language, but the designation given to high Chinese officials by Portuguese traders, who borrowed the word from Malay. The Malay word refers to a minister and, ironically, originates from the Sanskrit word, 'mantri'. Therefore, let us not teach our children Mandarin, but Chinese. There is nothing else to learn anyway because the same language is used as the official language of all Chinese speaking countries and geographical areas, such as the People's Republic, Taiwan, Hong Kong, Macau as well as Singapore. Cantonese is alive in Hong Kong and Hakka in Singapore and Malaysia, but the standard language is always Guoyu.

Chinese is a predominantly monosyllabic language. If a language is monosyllabic, it can have only a limited number of combination of sounds. It becomes quite a challenge to express all the ideas with such a limited number of words and sounds. The Chinese language expanded the vocabulary by using various tones, which are different ways of pronouncing the same sound. The number of tones has changed from time to time and from area to area. Modern Standard Chinese has four tones, a level tone, a rising tone, a falling and rising tone, and a falling tone, numbered from one to four in that order. Even with this refinement, the four hundred odd possible sounds can be increased to only about 1600. This means that there are innumerable words sounding absolutely alike, making spoken word rather difficult to understand. The Chinese use more than one word meaning the same thing augmented by gestures.

The way Chinese is transliterated into the Roman script by the fiat of the PRC is misleading in pronunciation, especially for us in India, whose languages have sounds quite similar to those in Chinese. Therefore, let us learn the correct pronunciation of Chinese sounds with the help of the Devanagari script.

Vowels: a, e (pronounced like the u in turn), i o, u (close to the German umlauted u).

Chinese is rich in consonants. Roman transliterations and Devanagari equivalents are:

g (क), k (ख), ng (ङ), j (च), q (छ), d (त), t (थ), n (न), b (प), p (फ), f (फ़), m (म), y (य), l (ल), w, x (श) but palatal as in Dravidian languages, sh (ष), s (स), h (ह), c (त्स), r (.ष) retroflex close to the sound in Tamil and Malayalam, z (pronounced as dz), ch (क्ष) and zh.

One hopes that this demonstrates how misleading the Roman transliteration is. One also hopes that if we teach Chinese in India, we will transliterate in Devanagari without the intermediation of the misleading Roman alphabets.

Chinese has virtually no grammar as words do not change forms, in fact, they cannot change forms through declensions and conjugations. The context is all in such a situation. The nouns have no gender. Therefore, once the four tones are mastered, Chinese is easy to speak. Writing is a different ballgame altogether, as thousands of characters have to be learnt. Therefore, those, who are planning to learn Chinese, should decide what they are going to use it for, and concentrate on speaking alone or both speaking and reading.

Chinese is naturally not spoken in a uniform manner all over that huge country. Over a period of time, the various speeches had diverged into mutually unintelligible languages. One could call Chinese a collection of languages. Something similar happened in India when spoken forms of Sanskrit evolved into different languages. The same thing happened in Europe when spoken Latin evolved into French, Spanish, Portuguese and Italian. Chinese did not break up like Latin and Sanskrit solely thanks to its writing system. A syllabic system like Sanskrit or use of alphabet as in Latin would have led to Chinese changing into several separate languages. But a picture means the same thing, no matter how it is pronounced and it retains the same meaning, no matter how the pronunciation changes over time. Thus, written Chinese united China as much as the imperial armies or the Confucian ethics. It united the country not only in space, but in time too because ancient texts can be read and understood without worrying about how the word was read centuries back – something impossible in any other part of the world. Now, the Chinese government is making the Beijing speech the common spoken language of the entire country – the ultimate triumph of centralisation.

Writing Chinese

The oldest Chinese writing is found in turtle bones used for making predictions. Paper came into use in the Han times and the shapes of ideographs also changed with the use of paper and ink. It also got petrified at that time and became unchangeable thereafter. While pronunciation went on changing, the writing remained frozen. This also happens, to some extent, in English where the spelling has remained unchanged for about 400 years, but pronunciation has changed. However, the difference is that, because English has an alphabet, new ideas and borrowed words can be written down with a fresh, almost infinite combination of letters. In Chinese, it meant that all thoughts, by necessity, had to be expressed through this way of writing and only this way. Words conveying new concepts cannot be borrowed, but expressed through existing symbols already carrying some meaning or by making up a new picture. While alphabet or syllabic writing can combine in an almost limitless manner to create any number of words, a new picture has to be associated arbitrarily with a sound. No wonder the number of ideographs swelled to more than 40,000 by the 17th century, making serious scholarship impossible for none, but the leisured class.

Chinese writing is truly the concrete depiction of objects they represent. It is very vivid, very visual, emphasising the aesthetic. Many ideographs bring out the sense of the word beautifully. 'Yue' meaning Moon is a stylised crescent. 'Zuo', the verb meaning sit shows two persons above the character for ground. East shows the sun amidst a tree, natural for people living far away from the sea. The combination of mother and child is 'hao', good. The character for 'thief' tells the whole story with two men, money, the Moon and a knife. 'Che' meaning cart is the wheel, cabin and axle as seen from above.

The beauty of such writing made calligraphy a highly prized art form and a companion to painting. Calligraphy became the training ground for painters. A famous calligrapher brought out the connection beautifully, "Every horizontal stroke is like a mass of clouds in battle formation, every hook like a bent bow of the greatest strength, every dot like a falling rock from a high peak, every turning of the stroke like a brass hook, every drawn out line like a dry vine of great old age, and every swift and free stroke like a runner at his start."[8]

Chinese Script and the Unity of China: Pluses and Minuses

Irrespective of the regional differences in spoken language, the script united China and kept it united. We have seen how the First Emperor unified the writing. Still, the language with tens of thousands of ideographs is hardly a vehicle for mass literacy. "It separated the classes, but united the regions" as Ross Terrill sums up.[9] In other words, it was a unity imposed from above with the use of instruments available only with the small elite and was, thus, an instrument of control and domination, just as was the Confucian ethics, which was neither a popular religion nor systematic philosophy, but a government sponsored code of conduct that froze social equations altogether and served the interests of the ruling elite. It was another element in the Chinese culture that led to the inexorable centralisation of Chinese political life. Another fallout from this reverence for the written word is that China never developed a tradition of public oratory, which is an essential ingredient in appealing to the masses, open debate of issues, the give and take of ideas as against the one way communication of the written word. *Ramayana* and *The Iliad* were chanted. The Buddha and Jesus preached. Socrates and our old philosophers debated. None of this has parallels in China. How much of this has contributed to the closed politics of China from time immemorial? How different is it from the attitude of the argumentative Indian? How have our habits and, by extension, systems of governance been influenced by this difference? A subject to ponder! No matter what our conclusion would be on that question, it is notable that China never had much of public speechmaking, press conferences or interviews with leaders. There is no direct communication with the demos, no mass rallies. In 1966, Mao appeared in eight rallies of the Red Guards, but never spoke a single word, although he issued several 'highest directives' in writing. Even now, leaders appear only to wave to the audience after the conclusion of the Party Congress or National Days, but never address the people. In China, there is no equivalent of the much anticipated speech by the Prime Minister from the ramparts of the Red Fort.

Countries around China, which had no script of their own, borrowed the Han writing when they first wrote their language, but it is telling that all of them have partially or fully given up reliance on Chinese script. Japanese, which is rich in declensions and conjugations and has a complex grammar, which is beyond the capacity of Chinese script to depict, created an extra set of syllabic writing, inspired by Sanskrit. It goes back to the 9th century and is attributed to a monk and Sanskrit scholar, Kukai. A wise ruler of Korea got rid of the Chinese script altogether and got it replaced with a syllabic script known as Hangul, a reform prompted by his noble wish to disseminate education to the widest extent among his people. The Vietnamese also did the same and used the Roman alphabet, though their language is even more rigidly monosyllabic than Chinese. Only Chinese remains imprisoned in picture writing.

Post-Revolutionary China tried gamely to struggle against this historic handicap and broad-base education. One measure undertaken was to follow in the footsteps of the First Emperor and simplify the script. The other was to make reporting in media to use no more than 1500 characters. This spread literacy but, probably, also dumbed down journalism, which did not worry the Communist party, which was more interested in propaganda than information and analysis.

How can a language so handicapped, so rooted in the culture and habits of one country that is so different from all others, and so impervious to external influences be touted as a potential global language? Presumably, by some who have not studied it.

Art and Architecture

We have already seen how the Shang people, the earliest known residents of China worked on pottery, bronze and jade to reach a great level of sophistication. Their buildings and the art contained there are all lost through fire, warfare, and natural calamities, but their tombs contain magnificent objects that began a glorious tradition sustained through centuries. The technical skill acquired by the Chinese in pottery and jade carving was never lost and they continued to produce the most beautiful objects throughout their history.

Painting was the medium through which Chinese artists expressed themselves the best. We have already seen how calligraphy was a prerequisite for painters. The best of Chinese painting was that of a landscape, which a gentleman of cultivated taste and leisure contemplated with mystic intensity and transferred to a silk scroll. The official credo of Confucianism did not provide for such contemplation, but the alternate teaching of Taoism, the meditative and quietist teaching of Laozi (लओत्से) offered scope for it, as it taught a way of life in which man moulded himself on nature, when one created harmony with nature by adapting oneself to nature's rhythms through non-assertion and 'actionless activity' in contrast to the call to obedience in the way of Confucius. The master of Tao taught, 'be subtracted and yet again be subtracted till you have reached non-activity. Then, through this non-activity, there will be nothing unaccomplished.' Inspired by this teaching, the Chinese painter immersed himself in nature, but came back to pick up the brush and silk screen to produce the deeply contemplative landscapes that are the greatest treasures of Chinese culture.

Chinese architecture was as closely earthbound as the painting. They never built soaring towers that tried to touch the sky or aspired to heaven like the Indian gopuram or the Gothic cathedrals, but constructed low-slung spread out buildings, roofs and eaves delicately carved like the brush strokes of a calligrapher. It avoided straight lines diligently. Gates have walls behind them, pavilions follow one behind the other, gardens never trimmed as in the West. The only towers built were Buddhist pagodas, which were, perhaps, inspired by Indian architectural ideas. There is one in Beijing, behind the Tiananmen (थियनआनमन) and the old Forbidden City on a small hill, to mark the visit of the fourth Dalai Lama to Beijing, a notable exception to the traditional plan of the city.

Buddhism and Arts

Buddhism, which also brought along certain concepts of portrait painting and architecture, left notable imprints in China. In

India, we are all taught in school that Fa Xian and Xuan Zang, who reached our country during the reigns of Chandragupta and Harshavardhana, respectively, were the most important Buddhist links with China. In fact, Buddhism had reached China and flourished there more than three centuries earlier. It is well known that the Mahayana branch of Buddhism developed in Gandhara, primarily by the great philosopher Ashvaghosha around the 1st century CE. The region called Afghanistan today and the adjoining areas of Central Asia were great centres of Buddhism in those days. We recall with pain the loss of the treasures of Bamiyan that were the great gifts to humanity from that area. Buddha was presented in image form in Gandhara and such images would, no doubt, have been sent to China even then. The sculpture of human forms developed in China under the inspiration of this art. Bronze images of the Buddha were made in China in large numbers, but hardly any exist now because most of them were destroyed or melted down when an officially sponsored campaign against Buddhism began a couple of centuries after the journey of Xuan Zang. We know about them only from the Korean and Japanese images of the same period. Buddhism reached Japan and Korea from China and is far more actively practiced in both countries today compared to China. There was another route for Indian influence to reach China, via South East Asia. The coastal areas of China, especially the provinces of Fujian and Guangdong, being trading regions, were in constant contact with South East Asia and, through them, with the South Indian empires. There is need for much more research on the intermediation of Indian culture by South Asian kingdoms in its impact on China.

Equally important was cave art in the style of Ajanta. Many small kingdoms in Northwest China established by invading non-Chinese groups (always described as 'barbarian' by the Chinese) in the interregnum between Han and Tang dynasties accepted Buddhism with enthusiasm. It was quite logical for them to do so because they were socially excluded groups, who had no sympathy for China's official credo and welcomed an alternative from another country. So also with Liao dynasty, who made many rock-cut caves with Buddha images. Such caves including the famous Tunhuang from the desert of Western China were discovered only in the 20th century. The desert caves were sealed airtight, therefore, they preserved their contents perfectly in the dry air. They have revealed the only genuine examples available of silk paintings of the Tang era.

While we appreciate that Buddhism was the only foreign influence on ancient China, we should also recognise that it was a dissident trend encouraged only by one dynasty, the Tang, and that too for a brief duration. Since then, Buddhism has existed in China as popular belief, more or less as a dissident counter current, at great variance from official preferences.

Absence of Epic and Drama

Just as sculpture would have remained a gap in Chinese artistic achievements, but for the Buddhist contributions, there are strange lacunae in Chinese literature too. Parallel to their intense contemplation of nature creating great landscapes, the Chinese wrote some of the most evocative lyric poetry on nature. But they never created an epic that evoked the collective memory of the people unlike us or the Greeks, no matter how pedestrian *The Iliad* is with its puppet characters casually manipulated by gods compared with the human passions and agonised choices depicted in the *Ramayana* or the *Mahabharata.*

So too with drama! We look in vain for an Aeschylus or Sophocles or a Bhasa or Kalidasa. One has to wait till the Mongol Yuan dynasty's time for drama to be performed on the stage and that too as popular art outside the ambit of official recognition. As Yuans were foreigners, many Chinese scholars abstained from serving them and retired from public life. It was this dissident set that created drama, plays with songs and dialogues in ordinary speech. We have a record of more than 1700 plays by more than 100 writers belonging to this period. It is an illustration of official hostility to such a popular art form that less than ten percent of the listed plays are available now and the official history of the Yuan makes no mention at all of the plays. No government in China had any interest in art that is not officially sanctioned.

This astonishing absence in an otherwise great literary tradition makes perfect sense when we recall some of the ideas on China that we have already encountered. The foundation of society in China was based on the concept of harmony based on adjustment in human relations for the greater good of the society. This arrangement deemphasises conflict, which is the lifeblood of epic and drama. At the same time, History was elevated by the Chinese to the level of the ultimate art form from where conclusions for contemporary living ought to be drawn. With such a corpus of texts of history, the need for epics vanished in China. History did the duty of what epics did in all civilisations, including the modern cultures inspired by the ancient. No matter what our political persuasions are, we evoke our epics. Lakshman Rekha and Shakuni Mama are all alive and well in India. After the Communist Ministry in Kerala was dismissed in 1959, a senior Minister, who was born a Christian, responded when asked about their future plans, 'we will meet in the Kurukshetra'. The battle between dharma and adharma engaged in Kurukshetra was as vivid and real to him as it was to Dr. Radhakrishnan, who evoked the same Kurukshetra in 1962 at the time of the Chinese invasion. On the other hand, Mao invoked the conflict between the kingdoms of Han and Chu prior to the war with India. In China, Clio, the Muse of History, absorbed and digested Calliope, Melpomene, Thalia and Polyhymnia, the Muses of Epic Poetry, Tragedy, Comedy, and Sacred Song.

Chinese Poetry

But Erato, the Muse of Lyric poetry and even Euterpe, the Muse of Erotic Poetry, flourished as nowhere else. They came into their own in the time of troubles, following the collapse of the Han when intellectuals migrated to Taoism. Poetry and painting came close together and attempted to capture the moment of revelation when the mind is immersed in nature. This contemplation and the nostalgic style that accompanied it became a staple of China. Though enormous amount of such lyrics were written over more than fifteen hundred years, the feel, ideas and style of expression hardly changed. In fact, it became a badge of honour to compose 'in the style of' some old poet. The poem would be much admired if it closely resembled a composition of the older writer in phrasing, mood and imagery. This extremely conservative tradition and custom was so strong that even Mao wrote 'in the style of' some classical writer or the other when it came to his poetry despite its revolutionary content. He celebrated revolutionary martyrs including his first wife by imagining that their souls are greeted by the goddess of the Moon, they are welcomed with cassia wine by a character in a legend, etc. Even the name he gave to his later wife, Jiang Qing, who became notorious during the Cultural Revolution, was an allusion to a poem by the famous writer Wang Wei of the Tang era. Why was there no evolution at all? Discussing this theme, T S Eliot, one of the greatest writers in English language in the 20th century, pointed out that the persistence of literary creativity in a people consisted of maintaining an unconscious balance between tradition that is contained in the past and originality among the living. D H Lawrence put the idea in different words, 'to carry on a tradition, you must add something to the tradition'. By this definition, the Chinese literary tradition went into stasis long back with only nifty refinements rather than real innovations. This parallels the changeless political and social equations of the Chinese empire.

Prose and Fiction

As we have already seen, history was the best example of ancient Chinese prose. Folk tales existed, but they were hardly deemed to be literature. The real scholarly thing was to write in the condensed classical style of the Qin or the Han times, a style utterly unintelligible to the masses. It survived only because the examination system that was streamlined during the Sui and Tang eras demanded that all candidates master it. The aim was to write an eight paragraph essay done within rigid parameters. The deadly influence of this antique and menacing 'eight legged essay' lingered on till imperial examinations themselves were abolished in early 20th century. Prose literature in colloquial speech arose during the Yuan era for the same reasons that produced popular drama, which we have already discussed. Popular fiction continued to flourish on the margin, free of the stamp of official authority, like *The Water Margin* translated with the telling title of *All Men are Brothers,* the 14th century adventure of enlightened bandits; *The Monkey,* the 16th century work narrating a fictionalised account of the travel of Xuan Zang to India; *Jin Ping Mei,* one of the best known pornographic works of all time, originally published anonymously for obvious reasons and frequently suppressed in China; and, finally, the marvellous *Dream of the Red Chamber* written in the 18th century about the decay of a noble family – all of which are widely read and much admired today.

How Developed was China Scientifically?

Small libraries have been written about all the things China invented; how much was invented, how it helped China progress, why all those inventions did not transform China into an industrialised society long time back, are useful questions to confront.

Like any old society, China had a lot of empirical knowledge in areas like agriculture, medicine, mathematics required for measurement, etc. We have seen how the First Emperor allowed the retention of only books of practical knowledge. We should realise that basic science that seeks to look for unifying principles that underlie phenomena, that tries to unify what appears to be multifarious, like the law of Gravitation or the Periodic Table is a quest that starts from the awe felt by the observer of the world and the urge felt by the observer to grasp these basic underlying principles. That is why a mathematical theorem is both correct and elegant and a scientific theory logical and beautiful. This awe is a spiritual feeling, though it has nothing to do with any established religion. In all high cultures, the study of phenomena and understanding their basic principles continued independent of current religious doctrines. 'No amount of assertion by the Vedas would make the fire feel cold' Adi Shankara declared in a brilliant definition of rationality. Science is a quest and not development of new techniques. As the Chinese who sedulously avoided questions about what lay beyond the phenomena, they did not make scientific discoveries as was done by the West since Renaissance. What China did well was technology and not science. They claim credit for four innovations – paper, printing, gunpowder and the magnetic compass – and display the assumed portraits of the four inventors in all schoolrooms, but all of them are technological innovations of great merit, but not scientific discoveries.

Progress in technology also does not necessarily mean social progress. Society progresses only when inventions and innovations are brought to bear for the benefit of the larger society. The Andeans knew the wheel, which they used for making children's toys, but did not apply to make a wheelbarrow because they thought that the slaves would be adequate to move stuff from place to place. That is the difference between ancient innovations and those made in Europe since the 17th century because, in the latter case, a social mechanism existed to transfer the benefit of the innovation to the whole society, which was absent in older societies. Paper and printing were Chinese inventions, but they were not put to use to promote mass literacy and empowerment of the people. The Chinese system just did not allow that even as an idea. But, when the moving type was developed in Germany, it was used not only to print the Bible in German so that the masses could read for themselves and, more dangerous for monopolists of power, think for themselves, leading to a religious revolution, but also to print and publish books in huge quantities on a vast variety of subjects, leading to inevitable economic and political revolutions. Europe, a collection of small countries much smaller than China, had 220 printing presses that had brought out more than eight million books by the year 1500. Though China claims credit for paper and printing, how many books did it publish on what variety of subjects by 1500, in the 15 centuries that elapsed after the inventions? What matters is not the invention, but the social milieu that puts the invention to best use, which China did not possess, leading to its backwardness.

Zheng He's Naval Expedition

This will also be the appropriate place to dispose of another much touted claim from China, the recently much written about voyages of Zheng He. This had always been treated in the past in China as an aberration and a curiosity until the Chinese government fanned it into a great example of China's long involvement in the Indian Ocean as part of its big power projection. They produced a movie, issued a stamp to mark the 600th anniversary of his first sailing and declared a 'Navigation Day' to pump up Zheng He as a great voyager. Western countries have collaborated in this exercise to boost China, of which the most blatant piece of evidence is the book on the Indian Ocean titled *Monsoon* by Robert Kaplan. Yong Le, the third emperor of the Ming dynasty, was suddenly inspired to do an expedition of the Southern Sea (South China Sea) and the Western Sea (Indian Ocean). He entrusted the work to Zheng He, a Mongol, who had served the Yuan dynasty in its last stronghold of Yunnan and offered his services to the Ming when he was captured, castrated and sent into the army. The Chinese official histories naturally described his expeditions as tribute collecting missions. But such an attitude would not do today when China has to present a peaceful face. Therefore, the whole thing was described in 2006 as a voyage to promote friendly relations among people. However, the countries visited by the Chinese remember things differently because Zheng He threatened and bullied and, in Kandy, kidnapped the ruler to extract tribute.

Though never attributed any significance even by the Chinese because these activities were strategically pointless forays undertaken and terminated at imperial whim, this effort is elevated by the current Chinese propaganda machinery as part of their endeavour to project their 'historical' role in the Indian Ocean. Zheng He arrived in the Kerala and Gujarat coasts, but this is not mercifully described as discoveries as Europeans once characterized Vasco da Gama's journey across the Arabian Sea when he was piloted by Indian sailors. Zheng He had the same kind of guidance from Indian sailors. He sailed one of the best chartered seas, whose routes and wind patterns had been described as early as the 1st century CE. How laboured and futile are the efforts to compare Zheng He, who left nothing in his wake to Columbus, who sailed an unknown sea! What an impact did those three little ships commanded by the Grand Admiral make on world history! In his slanted labour, Kaplan describes the utterly pointless foray as 'a great presence', which helped safeguard the flow of vital goods against pirates and was a 'demonstration of soft, benevolent power', claiming without any proof that Chinese withdrawal 'led to piracy on a large scale'. In his book, he makes ten references to Zheng He, who made only sporadic visits over a period of less than two decades, but is entirely silent on the long term naval presence of the South Indian emperors that generated immense cultural influence in countries to our East; the mutually beneficial exchanges with Arab countries, promoted by rulers of India's west coast that kept the sea safe for everybody including Zheng He's fleet, till the Portuguese arrived to wreak havoc on peaceful coexistence of all religions and mutually profitable trade. Evidently, history is being manufactured with a motive. At some point, the Chinese even produced a map, which hinted at a voyage by Zheng He eastward implying that he could well have reached America well before Columbus, but this was such a blatant fake that it had to be abandoned quickly. This is a typical example of China study by a Western scholar, who works with an agenda, a repeated phenomenon that we in India should be wary of and not fall into critical acceptance.

A Recapitulation

We have now reviewed the history of China, the major elements of its culture and how they came to be, how it has been governed, and how the country dealt with other countries and neighbours during the imperial days. It may be too short and, therefore, not as detailed as such an immense country with an immense history and culture deserves, but still a good basis for our purposes. Before we try to have a look at how China changed in the 20th century, it could be of help if we recapitulate the most salient elements in the argument thus far.

1. China was united as one administrative unit by the Qin and the Han Dynasties and has basically remained intact as a political entity, notwithstanding periodic collapse of regimes and fairly prolonged intervals of turmoil and divisions into small states warring with each other.

2. China's unity was underpinned by homogeneity of race, a written language using ideographs that overcame dialect and language differences, an official ideology based on the teachings of Confucius, which was adopted by governments and imposed on the country to create homogeneity of culture and literary norms, centralised bureaucracy trained in official ideology and loyalty to the ruler.

3. Chinese cultural and political habits were set before the country came into contact with any other civilisation, thus making it a rare species of culture that reached full bloom uninfluenced by any other and, therefore, not amenable to changes due to other cultural influences.

4. As a result of this homogeneity and unity, the primary objective of governance in China was the welfare of the society as a collective.

5. More than any other civilisation, China honoured history as a guide to action, using it where legends, epics and religious parables would be used in other cultures.

6. As a country that had little contact with other entities with comparable level of culture, China had scant experience of normal foreign relations, which left it ill-prepared to cope with the aggressive push of the West in the 19th century.

Chapter VI

China and the West

Two types of westerners came to China in modern times, the Missionary and the Merchant.

The Missionary wanted to recruit China to his cause, originally his religion, but other causes too have found their missionaries since then. The original Missionary naturally saw the largest 'heathen' country, the most fertile of potential fields for his labour, and therefore worked with might and main. For other kinds of missionaries of the secular variety, who have appeared in recent times, propagating their economic or political faith and converting China is the grandest of all prizes. That makes China the most important object for the missionaries of both Communism and international capitalism, to be wooed, studied, admired, coaxed, cajoled, to ingratiate oneself with and, ultimately, recruit to one's side so that its weight and greatness benefit his side and come to his aid in his ideological and physical combats.

The pioneer and archetype of the Missionary was a real missionary, the Jesuit priest, Matteo Ricci, who arrived in Beijing with the objective of converting the Chinese to the true faith. His strategy was to try to convert the Court and through them, the whole country, convincing them of the truth of his religion through the instrument of the teaching of Confucius himself. Another item in his armoury was the skill in mathematics and astronomy possessed by him and his fellow monks. He learned Chinese, dressed like a Court official, took the Chinese name of Li Matou and worked for the Emperor. The Chinese accepted his technical knowledge, improved their calendar and ignored his preaching. This established the pattern of China's dealings with the West – improving their skills with borrowed technology while remaining impervious to ideas, worldviews and beliefs of the outsiders who brought those skills. The Chinese were intellectually self sufficient as inheritors of an autonomously formed and comprehensively articulated way of life. They did not need any imported philosophy. From the Jesuits of the 17th century to the Marxists of the 20th century and the capitalists of the 21st century, they were only interested in the technological improvements that would add to the comforts of the Chinese way of life and not introduce any change to that way of life itself. It was for the Chinese to select what to imbibe and what to reject. Just as the Chinese took the calendar and rejected Christianity, they took technology and knowhow from the Soviet Union and the West while rejecting the proletarian theories of the former and democracy of the latter as incompatible with Chinese ethos. Ricci died in Beijing in 1610 without converting the Chinese, but only after introducing Confucius to the Western world as the perfect thinker, who created the basis for a harmonious society – the seeds of fascination with China, admiration for its 'greatness' and 'superior culture', the keenness to see that country through rose-tinted glasses of respect and optimism that has haunted the West ever since.

The Merchant saw the hugest market once the industrial Revolution generated mass produced goods that needed new markets. In the beginning, he did no better than the Missionary as illustrated by the much-quoted letter from the Qian Long (छियन लुङ) Emperor to the English monarch, which brusquely dismissed the possibility that China could need any product of alien fabrication and doubted that foreigners were capable of ever acquiring even the rudiments of his country's civilisation. Diplomatic approach failed, but that was followed by the battering ram. The so called Opium Wars forcibly opened China for trade, identified ports where Chinese law ceased to operate and divided China into quasi-colonial spheres of influence of various Western powers. The Missionary and the Merchant became allies at this point. When missionaries were attacked, further trade concessions were demanded as compensation; trading areas became bases for missionaries to preach in safety and security. Trading posts where Chinese law ceased to operate also became refuges for rebels against the regime to preach new ideas like adoption of western technology, nationalism and the overthrow of the empire to save China using western ideas. However, the coalition of the Missionary and the Merchant harmed them both in the long run because such an alliance was unacceptable to the Chinese. The Missionary was distrusted because he was preaching under the protection of the exploitative Merchant and the Merchant lost business and respect because he was seen as helping push an alien teaching instead of just doing business. This expression of suspicion and distrust applied even to the secular missionaries, who went to China with the message, first of Marxism and then of democracy, free market and free trade. They found that the Chinese took the technology, but rejected the alien theories. Yet, the hope that China could be converted did not easily die in the heart of any of the missionaries, religious preachers, left ideologues, and free market globalisers, luring them like the smile of the temptress into greater and greater investment of time and effort, emotions and wealth in the China project.

China's Reaction to the West: How to Save China?

By the second half of the 19th century, it was clear to the intellectuals in China that reforms were urgently required if their nation was to be saved. Unlike in other countries, intellectuals were also administrators in China because they alone had the leisure to study for the examinations, which were the sole path to government positions and also because it was their Confucian duty to serve the state. As administrators, Confucian ethics also enjoined that they should be exemplars for the public. Therefore, the analysis of the reasons for China's decline was undertaken by the intelligentsia not just as an academic exercise, but simultaneously also as a plan of action on behalf of the ruling elite for the regeneration and strengthening of the ancestral land. Debates on what ailed China and the prescriptions for its cure raged in China all the way till the success of the Communist revolution in 1949. This debate has not come to an end even today. Therefore, unlike in other countries, academic debates on development strategies are also political conflicts in China. That is why the Great Leap Forward launched by Mao in 1959 as an attempt to fast track China into the league of industrialized nations and the Great Proletarian Cultural Revolution launched by him in 1965-66 to cleanse the Party of deviant thinking were also struggles of ideas and not merely political struggles about removing his foes from positions of power.

The next salient point is that China conducted this debate only vis a vis the West and its multifarious instruments of power and pressure. Other parts of the world just did not enter the picture. This is sometimes interpreted in India as something of a slight that China does not care for comparison with anybody, not even with the West (identified with the USA in the present circumstances); that China conceives of a hierarchy of nations in which India ranks low, etc. This is not quite fair. The entire gamut of premises on which China's culture and, hence, its governing system rested was challenged and threatened only by the West and the will of the Chinese nation was to deal with this challenge. The persistence of this point of view could be seen in the neat and pithy observation of Deng Xiaoping that the G 7 was no different from the group of countries that imposed unequal treaties on China. Therefore, we should take with seriousness the repeated statements of Chinese leaders and spokesmen about an Asian future and the place of both India and China in that world. We, in India, did nothing of the sort that was done by any state that calls itself 'West'. No one else did anything of the sort. It was therefore natural for them to be obsessed with the ideologies and activities of precisely those, who threatened their age old ethos and not be distracted by other issues. This also explains the general indifference of China to developing country issues as an academic subject, their aloof position in the UN on the questions of development where their contribution in debates and ideas is negligible in contrast with the significant engagement of India, both politically and in the realm of ideas. Their constant, almost obsessive, comparisons with the USA and attempts to demonstrate that they can do some things better than the United States also derives from these historic concerns.

The First Prescription: Save China's Spirit, Use West's Knowhow

The bottom line for the first generation of intellectuals cum administrators, who faced this question was to save China's tradition and culture while making it strong enough to protect itself. It was interesting that military modernisation and strengthening was thought of as top priority by the Chinese in contrast with Indian modernisers, who concentrated on social reform and industrial self reliance as preconditions even for the achievement of independence and virtually ignored military power. It was natural that they considered Confucian thought to be the core of Chinese culture. The only concession to be made to the West, they thought, was the requisitioning of the needed technology for the military defence of China. The earliest reformers took 'self-strengthening' as their theme. The best expression of this quest was the thesis developed by the late 19th century thinker Liang Qichao (ल्याङ छी क्षऔ), who propounded the theory that China should unite its 'ti' (थी) or 'spirit' with Western 'yung' (युङ) or practical knowhow. Both the concepts go back to Mencius, but the great sage saw the two concepts as fully correlated, with the second emerging organically from the first rather than being grafted to it. In other words, the 'spirit' or the ethos should not be compromised by the practical instruments for action. This was a valid and viable position to take when, as in the time of Mencius, China did not have to contend with any alternative ideology or philosophy of governance, but in the late 19th century, there is bound to be a conflict between the protection of China's 'spirit' and means of action imported from abroad. This organic link was missed by the later thinkers. Introduction of alien technology, military or civilian, brings with it other elements of the exporting culture that are parts of its 'spirit'. Therefore, the argument that China could preserve its ancient ethos and social relations while accepting western technology was a fallacy, but the siren's song of this short cut continued to lure the Chinese for long. There were frequent debates about 'red' vs. 'expert', shorthand for those, who act with total commitment to ideological correctness vs. those who pay attention to practical results and ignore the purity of ideology – an updated version of 'ti' vs. 'yung' – during the Communist times that are incomprehensible to outsiders, but were motivated by the very Chinese obsessions we have already studied. It is also not an accident that the 'Four Modernisations' of China, originally proposed by Zhou Enlai in 1975 and subsequently made official policy by Deng Xiaoping (तङशिआओ फिङ), deal exclusively with technological modernization and avoid social and political issues. Here again, we can note and appreciate the difference in priorities with India. It is ironic that even the leadership claiming to be Marxist could not free itself of the traditional China they claimed to have rejected in toto and the urge to hold on to what is felt to be unique in that country proved too entrenched to discard.

This also explains certain features in China's current intellectual climate. As we have already seen, China has little academic interest in developing countries. In the 1970s, they claimed that they represented Asia in the UN Security Council and were the voice of the developing countries. That was the time when some of the idealism of the Maoist revolution still lingered. Now, the talk is only about China being a big power. The domestic counterpart of this indifference to the developing world is the lack of concern for ethnic minorities. The government was so blind to this aspect that, when children from minority nationalities were paraded in their distinct dresses during the 2008 Olympics, every child paraded was of Han nationality dressed in the traditional manner of a minority.

On the other hand, the USA gets all the attention for a combination of reasons. For the 'yung' activists, that was the place to go. For the super-patriots, that is the country to take on to prove that it is China that is the centre of the world once again. There is a third group of intellectuals, who evolved into the 'New Left' of the 1980s, critics of the regime's pro-US policies. Survivors of the Cultural Revolution, who were lucky to resume studies when colleges reopened in China in 1975, they are the only set with genuine knowledge of the Chinese countryside because they were sent to the countryside by Mao after 1969, where they remained at least till 1976, when their first batch was allowed to write college entrance examinations and leave the countryside if accepted for higher studies. Many of them studied in the USA and became interested in democracy and used that to critique the government. Research on the scope of democracy in China, a subject of extensive discussion in China that is barely noticed in India, is also the intellectual territory of this group.

Content of Chinese Nationalism

The second fallout of the impact of the West on China was the emergence of nationalism in China. We have already shown how China of the classical age had no nationalist postures. China was 'tianxia' or everything under the Sun where the just rule of the emperor attracted admiration and obedience from the entire world. There was no need for patriotism that unites those of a nation to confront those from another competing entity because such an entity that did not accept the Emperor as the supreme ruler was just inconceivable. Nationalism wore an anti-Manchu face in the beginning, because China declined under them, and because those rulers were redefined as foreigners. As the Manchus had become entirely sinified in the three centuries of their rule, there was a touch of Han racism in this line of attack, another strand of thinking that has persisted since then and, perhaps, has strengthened in recent times. Nationalism also compelled them to accept that they too were a 'guo', one among the many, (recall the 'warring States when China was divided into small entities, all described thus) however reluctantly. China acknowledges that there are many states, all theoretically equal, but is still not entirely comfortable in groupings of states.

Nationalism was extremely controversial among the young reformers of early 20th century. They argued that a nationalist would admire China's past, that was after all his own country's past, the past that reformers wanted to disown and eradicate. These intellectually alienated groups felt that nationalism would bring in old traditions by the back door. That group also rejected westernisation because that was seen as the sure way for the destruction of China. No wonder what was left as the default option for the modernizing Chinese was Communism that had the added attraction of having triumphed just then in Russia. It was also natural that it gathered more and more adherents among the intelligentsia, going from strength to strength till it captured power in 1949.

Communism and Old China

Even then, old China fought back. The strongest communist advocate of internationalism, one of the founders of the Chinese Communist Party, Chen Duxiu (क्षन तूशेयो) was expelled from the Party less than a decade after the Party came into being at Shanghai in 1921. The man who engineered the expulsion was Mao Zedong, an intellectual all right, but schooled exclusively in traditional Chinese scholarship and entirely devoid of the international perspective of the communists of that era. We have already seen how Mao saw the right of rebellion advocated by Mencius as the core teaching of Marx and how he wrote theoretical essays on Marxism and became the undisputed leader of the Party without mastering Marx's writings. The Chinese have treated all this as quite natural and have always asserted that his theories, described as 'Mao Zedong Thought' was as Chinese as it was thoroughly

Marxist and that it was entirely valid and relevant as it integrated the theory of Marxism with the practice of Chinese revolution.

From Empire to Republic

As had happened with every deteriorating dynasty, the Qing Empire was also plagued with rebellions from mid-19th century. But the situation of China was different from the time of the earlier dynasties because the new 'barbarians' possessed superior heavy artillery and arrived by sea, both beyond China's experience till then. The deadly combination of a collapsing internal situation, external pressure from the kind of superior military forces that China had never encountered earlier, and increasing alienation of intelligentsia led to the collapse of the government in 1911. Troops had rebelled in Wuhan on October 10, 1911 and declared a republic with Dr. Sun Yatsen as President. The emperor, a six year old boy, abdicated on February 12, 2012, thus bringing to an end the empire with the longest recorded history.

The boy emperor Pu Yi had a strange future. He kept his court more or less intact during the Republican days as the Chinese still could not abandon the old tradition that allowed the overthrown dynasty to retain imperial trappings. It was the populist General and warlord Feng Yuxiang, who finally disbanded the court of Pu Yi in the 1920s. Pu Yi fell into the hands of the Japanese invaders, who created the puppet kingdom of Manchuko in Northeast China and made him the king there. When that area was captured by the communists, they took him away, put him through ideological re-education and made him earn his keep as a gardener. He survived till 1967 and felt the worst of the Cultural Revolution before dying at the age of 61. A life that encapsulates all that China went through in those six decades!

What about the republic that was born a few years after the unfortunate Pu Yi? It had a similar fate, stripped of its aura, captured by its enemies and violently reshaped according to the will of the victorious communists. Let us remember that China was the first republic in Asia, reaching its centenary in 2012, an anniversary strangely ignored in China. It became a republic when only France, Switzerland and Liberia existed as republics outside the western hemisphere. But what happened was scary for anybody, who cared for China's future as a united country. Provinces declared independence; warlords controlled various regions. When Sun Yatsen resigned in favour of Yuan Shikai, a General in the service of the imperial government, in a desperate effort to unify the country, the latter quickly planned his own coronation as emperor. He died soon after, before the planned coronation. It was not surprising that the strongest leaders to emerge from this mess, Chiang Kai-shek and Mao Zedong, both plumped for authoritarian regimes underpinned by military support and willingness to use military power domestically to protect their power. The democratic idea fell on barren soil and struggled to sprout; it made repeated attempts only to wither.

A Republic but no Democracy

A brief digression on attempts at democracy in China may be relevant at this point. Elections were held in 1912-13, soon after the empire collapsed. Only males, who were taxpayers, had property, and had at least primary level education could vote. Monks, policemen, and opium addicts were among those who were disenfranchised. Still, 20 million peopled voted, a 50 percent turnout. Not bad as elections go even today! So far, this is the only national level election held in China, even on a limited franchise. By 1918, when World War I ended, almost three dozen countries had some kind of voting and women were on the threshold of achieving the right to vote in the USA and the UK, but China lost its way and fell prey to dictatorship and civil war. After the communist capture of power, there were local elections on universal franchise in which 278 million votes were cast. This coincided with the second wave of democracy in the world, but China, once again, aborted the process in favour of political struggle against the so called rightists and to carry out the disastrous Great Leap Forward, which led to mass starvation on a scale unheard of in the modern times. The third wave of democracy in the world in the 1970s and 80s also failed in China, once again, when the first Tiananmen Incident of 1976 following the death of Premier Zhou Enlai fizzled out and the next campaign that began with the 'Democracy Wall' and culminated with the demonstrations at the Tiananmen Square was suppressed violently on June 3-4, 1989 (Incidentally, though it is commonly called the Tiananmen Square incident, it was not an isolated event and was the most prominent part of anti-government demonstrations in hundreds of cities in China in which more than hundred million people took part – more than ten percent of the population coming out which compares quite impressively with anything seen in eastern Europe or Arab countries).[10]

Alternatives to authoritarianism failed to develop in China partly because the strong state resorted to determined use of force. We have seen how China had always had a very centralised and 'hard' system, which governed with the help of a committed bureaucracy. This is not a situation conducive to democracy. Luck also was with the system. Strongmen running Spain, Taiwan and Russia died when the ferment for change was seizing those countries in the 1970s, leaving a political vacuum, opening the door for generational change and political reform. However, when the first demonstration took place at Tiananmen after the death of Zhou Enlai in 1976 and the event was repeated on a larger scale in 1989, potential reformers were removed. Deng Xiaoping, the strongman stayed in power and ensured that no generational change took place except as planned by him. This happening and his use of all the force necessary to suppress the potential 'Chinese Spring' left the system stronger than ever.

The net result is that more than 50 percent of the global population, who are not able to elect their leaders by direct votes, live in China. It is also the largest segment of humanity with no free press and no right to organise political parties. What causes this situation? Why is the Chinese peasantry described by the eminent economist Hu Angang as "the world's biggest population without political representation"? How do we square that with 'China's rise'? To arrive at some sober conclusions, one has to look at China's social and economic policies since the 1949 Liberation.

Chapter VII

China after Liberation

The political history of China since Liberation is made to appear as a steady and straight-forward march towards a great future under the same single government providing continuity because the Communist Party had been in power all along and political succession has been determined by the secret inner councils of the Party without the uncertainties of democracy. This is unfortunately not true. What we have is a series of government changes carried out violently in the absence of open debate and periodic consultation with the people. The first ten years of the People's Republic were stable and peaceful, with steady growth of the economy. Then came the Great Leap Forward launched by Mao. The campaign failed, partly because it was too ambitious and also because the factions in the Party that did not agree with Mao sabotaged it by non-cooperation and obstruction. Mao lost the Presidency of the country primarily because of the failure of that campaign. He was succeeded by Liu Shaoqi (ल्यो षऔ छी) while Mao continued to lead the party. This unstable division of power could not last. It was upset when Mao launched the Cultural Revolution, which was primarily aimed at the Party leadership and their work methods. This campaign that began in 1966 played havoc with the Party and the government, leading to the disgrace and death of innumerable Party cadres and massive disruption in the work of every organisation and enterprise in the country. Normal governance began to be restored from 1969, which was followed by

China reaching out to the USA. The allies of Mao were purged soon after his death in 1976. The former Secretary-General of the Party, Deng Xiaoping assumed power and changed the way China was run by abolishing people's communes that collectivised agriculture and granting freedom to the peasants to cultivate as they wished, opening the economy for foreign investments through exclusive Economic Zones, and normalisation of relations with the USA. Thus, we can see at least six separate government changes in China between 1949 when the People's Republic was established and 1979 when 'reforms' were inaugurated by Deng, all accomplished with a strong dose of violence in the absence of democratic consultations—i) the government led by Mao between 1949 and 1959 with a basically united Communist Party that worked to establish peace, improve living standards across the board, develop close relations with the Soviet Union and articulate solidarity with the 'Third World'; ii) a brief period of upheaval in 1959-60 with the collapse of relations with the Soviet Union when Mao experimented with the 'Great Leap Forward' and lost his position in the government; iii) the period between 1960 and 1966 when Liu Shaoqi and Deng Xiaoping ran the country with Mao in relative eclipse; iv) the 1966-69 period of political chaos also reflected in China's foreign policy of hostility to both the USA and the Soviet Union and support for destabilization of governments in the neighbourhood; v) the 1969-75 period when Zhou Enlai and senior Party and military cadres restored normal administration, opened to USA to remedy China's isolation achieved in the previous half decade while being violently anti-Soviet; and, finally, vi) the successor government, which took full control by late 1976 after the death of Mao and the removal from power of his close allies, the Gang of Four and pushed for full normalization of relations with the USA and also opened up China's economy through 'reforms' as a process that went in coordination with the progress and expansion of its relations with the USA, simultaneously setting up rules for running the government that have been observed faithfully so far. It can be seen that policies changed sharply on each occasion and this made it quite hard for its own people to cope and for foreign countries to deal with China.

Since then China has grown steadily except for a period of time around the political upheaval in 1989. That major crisis was used by Deng to make personnel changes and to lay down procedures for periodic changes in the leadership in future. Senior leadership would retire at 70. The President and Premier would be chosen in such a manner that they could serve for ten years after working as the second in command position for at least one term. The President would also be the leader of the Party and the head of the Military Commission that has the final authority over the armed forces. These arrangements made political changes reasonably predictable even when carried out away from public gaze within the small group of leaders, a vast improvement when we recall that every man at the apex of power in China from the Guang Xu Emperor, who was poisoned to death in 1906, has been violently removed from power. During the days of the empire, there were only palace intrigues, but changes in the People's Republic were accompanied by mass violence organized with the forced involvement of most of the population, bringing much misery and deprivation in its wake and huge disruption of economic activity. Transfer of power became a routine non-event only when Xi Jinping (शी चिनफिङ) and Li Keqiang (ली खेछियाङ) took over as President and Premier respectively in 2012. Finally, the ordinary citizens were spared the usual orgy of violence on such occasions even if the entire process still excluded their involvement.

Achievements of China after Liberation

Liberation was genuinely popular and people could justifiably consider the regime 'our government', as they usually did in the 1950s, for the first time in the history of China. The leadership was mostly of peasant origin and had deep knowledge of rural China where the vast majority of people lived at that time. Nearly 80 percent of Party members were of peasant and worker origin. Therefore, the government was truly close to the people and truly committed to the betterment of the lives of poor peasants. In the first decade of the People's Republic, genuine all round growth was achieved. Grain output rose by 35 percent between 1952 and 1957, while it increased only by two percent per annum in the next 20 years, barely keeping pace with increasing population. Community medical schemes covered nearly 90 percent of the country. Life expectancy rose from 57 in 1957 to 68 in 1978 (It reached 71 only in 2000, which provides some support to the argument that China made superior gains in the social field in the early years of Mao compared to the so called liberalised era). Infant mortality fell from 139 in 1954 to 20 in 1980. China had an annual growth rate of nine percent in the first decade after Liberation, an impressive record even from the low base of the days of invasion and civil war. The introduction of simplified writing and attention to rural healthcare and education saw a great increase in literacy too. In fact, the real credit for the lead China has over India in social indicators actually goes to the Mao era when a large gap opened up from comparable starting points.

At the same time, it should also be emphasised that the story of social indicators in the reform era tell a different story. During that time, India had done as well or even better than China in relative movement. The gap remains, but that is still due to the lead gained by China in the early days of socialism and equality. Less discussed, but worth equal notice is the work done for the equality of women after Liberation. It was the women of China, who enjoyed the fruits of Liberation the most. The government suppressed prostitution and other forms of violence against women, another area where, sadly, there has been a grave slide back in recent times as police and military run brothels; there are more than 10 million sex workers; and keeping mistresses in the pre-Revolution style has become prevalent among ranking Party cadres.

Soviet Union and Hong Kong – Two Supports for China's Progress

China had two unique advantages at that time that were not replicated in any other developing country. Though not at all talked about now, the Soviet Union extended considerable amount of technical assistance to China in the 1950s, one of the largest programs of aid and transfer of technology in history. As many as 158 industrial complexes were built with Soviet help in the 1950s. The second was the existence of Hong Kong, through which China earned foreign exchange just by supplying what was their own population with the basic necessities of life. Food and even water sold to Hong Kong earned China foreign currency. China even ensured that Hong Kong was not included in the list of colonies maintained by the UN and its situation was not debated in the General Assembly as part of the annual review of decolonisation. The sophisticated financial centre in Hong Kong and its modern port and airport developed by others also served China without its government having to take any responsibility for their running. The existence of Hong Kong as an independent entity was and continues to be a crucial and unique factor for economic development of China, an advantage that no other country possessed or will possess. Indian analysts have not factored in the benefits derived by China from the huge technical assistance and the benefits from Hong Kong while comparing India and China, thus, seriously compromising the usefulness of their conclusions and recipes for action by us. Therefore, imitating China had its limits that were not fully understood.

China Loses Its Way

We have already seen how China grew impressively and made significant progress in social indices in the first few years after Liberation. But it hit a wall by 1958. The leadership cast about for fresh ideas and plans; their differing ideas led to a showdown within the Party during those years with leaders like Liu Shaoqi arguing for mechanisation of agriculture and Mao advocating decentralisation down to village level. This was the point at which Mao forced the Party to launch the Great Leap Forward, the ultimately disastrous campaign, meant to force-march China into the developed world. The failure and the ensuing sufferings of the people eclipsed Mao temporarily (he famously groused to his American friend Edgar Snow about his Party colleague, Deng Xiaoping, 'look at that shortie! He treats me like his dead parent whose funeral he is attending'), as he plotted revenge by launching his even more disastrous Cultural Revolution.

When things died down after the crescendo of violence from 1966 to 1968, the condition of China was clear to what was left of the leadership after a large portion was purged and violently dealt with. Even one of the Marshals of the People's Liberation Army (PLA) acknowledged later that the widespread violence of the '60s led to the death of more than 20 million people. Independent estimates by demographers have proved that deaths caused by the famine following the Great Leap Forward alone were between 30 and 50 million people. Nothing was built in cities in those years. People educated abroad, who responded to the leaders' appeal and returned to work for the country were attacked and reviled, first in the anti-rightist campaign of the late 50s and then during the Cultural Revolution. The first person, who was killed during the Cultural Revolution, was a school principal in Beijing called Bian Zhongyuan, who was beaten to death by her students, a shocking thing anywhere, but unthinkable in a culture that venerated teachers beyond the respect offered in any other culture. This was no way to earn loyalty.

Armed Forces Enter Politics

The period beginning 1959 also saw an extremely unhealthy political development – the intrusion of the Armed Forces into the centre of politics and government quite in violation of Mao's dictum that politics should be in command. After Mao was heavily criticised for the misguided Great Leap Forward, he leaned on the support of the military commanders in the Party Central Committee to protect his position. As time passed, the PLA became the only power centre available to him. Because of the tensions over Taiwan and the confrontation with the USA, and confrontation with the Soviet Union later, the PLA also got huge budgetary allocations. Minority areas were, for practical purposes, colonized by the PLA. For example, in Xinjiang 15 percent of the population consisted of the PLA Production and Reconstruction Corps, which raised 40 percent of the region's cotton and farmed 30 percent of the province's arable land. The PLA sent hundreds of thousands to offer logistical help to Vietnam during the American war there, and sent weapons to various guerrilla movements in Asia and Africa that violated the doctrine of peaceful coexistence and seriously distorted China's foreign policy by its incitement to destabilization and aggravation of tensions in its immediate neighbourhood and beyond. By 1969, uniformed personnel occupied half the seats in the Politburo, a distortion of domestic politics and diplomacy that took more than two decades to remedy.

Turnaround in Policy Towards the West

The real starting point for China's turn towards the West was the decision made by Mao to invite Nixon to visit China. We have seen how China hit a wall from the development point of view by 1958. At the same time, they also broke with the Soviet Union and were left with no friend, deprived of economic aid and with no significant economic links with any major power. China was not a member of the UN and its agencies, such as GATT, IMF, or The World Bank. At that time, there were not even 50 countries with embassies in Beijing, none but Cuba from the Western Hemisphere; none of the original five states, who founded the ASEAN; none from the Islamic world stretching from Pakistan to Mauritania, except Afghanistan, Pakistan, Iraq, Syria, Algeria, Morocco and Egypt. A major element in China's foreign policy at that time – something forgotten now and carefully ignored by the Chinese media and academics – was their shrill support for all kinds of armed guerrilla movements, and constant calls for the overthrow of established governments. That was why worry about Chinese intentions was the original motive for the setting up of the ASEAN. China's foreign policy at that time was incendiary, destabilising and provocative. The bizarre call by Zhou Enlai in Algiers in 1964 that 'Africa was ripe for revolution' was a remarkable example of this wayward policy that only made China lose friends and generated deep suspicions about its intentions.

It was also clear that the policy was not working. The coup attempted by the Indonesian Communist Party, the largest pro-Chinese Party at that time in the world, in 1965 was brutally suppressed by the armed forces. That is why Vietnam became the key for China as success in Vietnam would have emboldened China to expand its policy of destabilizing neighbours. If so, why did China execute a 180 degree turn and invite Nixon to the extreme annoyance of Vietnam? The answer most probably is that the Americans stayed on in South Vietnam long enough for the other South East Asian nations to politically unite to form ASEAN and gain the strength to protect themselves against internal subversion. Mao accepted as much when he told the North Vietnamese in 1971 that they would not be able to sweep out the Americans from South Vietnam just as China was not able to sweep out the Americans from Taiwan. Meanwhile, China had antagonised the Soviet Union sufficiently to get itself caught in a pincer between the two superpowers. That was why China reacted almost hysterically to the invasion of Czechoslovakia by the Soviet Union in 1968, fearing that it could be their turn next. The leadership feared that they faced strategic encirclement and defeat.

There is evidence that Mao identified the situation correctly and responded with characteristic boldness to make strategic decisions. He asked four Marshals of the PLA to prepare a position paper, which recommended an opening to the USA. Mao told his personal physician, "We have the Soviet Union to the north and the west, India to the south and Japan to the east. If all our enemies unite, attacking from the north, south, east and west, what do you think we should do?" Mao himself supplied the answer by pointing out that one allies with the distant country to fight the enemy who is closer and quoted the classic novel, *The Water Margin.*[11] It followed that the hand had to be extended to the USA. What followed later under Deng Xiaoping was only the logical and inevitable consequence of Mao's momentous strategic turn. Mao also rationalised his volte-face by declaring that the USA had never occupied any part of China and that, in any case, he liked rightists like Nixon, who said and did the same thing unlike the leftists, who say one thing and do something else. It was thus that China resumed contacts with the USA through its embassies at Warsaw in 1969, which culminated in Nixon's visit in 1972.

While there were twists and turns in China's domestic politics in the next decade, relations with the USA were steady, reaching full diplomatic relations on January 1, 1979, under Jimmy Carter, a Democrat, proof that the US strategy was bipartisan, based on political consensus, and that it was the Americans, who dictated the pace of evolution of relations with China. Once again, Vietnam became the key. Deng Xiaoping made an official visit to the USA soon after the normalisation of relations and China's attack on Vietnam took place soon after. Deng notified Carter of their intention to attack. Though Carter says in his memoirs of his presidency that he was shocked by this warning, the Americans and the Chinese maintained continuous contacts during the war and the Chinese ambassador met the US National Security Advisor every day while the war was on (On the other hand, Foreign Minister Vajpayee cut short his visit to China on hearing about this attack and returned home and Prime Minister Morarji Desai issued a statement criticising it). No interpretation of this bizarre and pointless war, which did no credit to China militarily, morally or politically, is possible except that China wanted to demonstrate to the USA that it was in the right camp. Wang Hui, a Chinese social scientist, explains this precisely, "The Open Door policies of Deng Xiaoping demanded a much deeper insertion of China into the world market. How did this happen? A key in this process was China's invasion of Vietnam .... The only reason for this otherwise senseless attack on a small neighbour was Deng's desire for a new relationship with the United States. The invasion was offered as a political gift to Washington and became China's entrance ticket to the world system. Here too, violence was the precondition of a new economic order."[12] This was not the only example of China's erratic behaviour at that time. One year earlier, the Chinese President had visited Congo ruled by Mobutu and the Shah of Iran well after his troops shot and killed hundreds in the centre of his capital – awful things for a communist to do. The Vietnamese, as usual, read the Chinese accurately even as the Chinese were getting ready to welcome Nixon. The Chinese embassy used to hold an annual party to mark the Chinese New Year. Not a single Vietnamese turned up in the 1972 reception held just before Nixon's visit. Zhou Enlai landed in Hanoi to brief the Vietnamese after the visit. When he began his briefing on exchanges with Nixon on Vietnam, a Politburo member retorted, 'Vietnam is our country, not yours. You have no right to say anything about it. You have no right to discuss this issue with the United States.' – an extraordinarily courageous thing to say when Vietnam depended so much on China in their resistance to the Americans.[1]. The attitude of the Vietnamese and the observation of the eminent Chinese critic should encourage us to have another perspective on China's economic strategy that was the fruit of the opening to the USA.

Western Agenda for China and How the Chinese Leadership Helps in Its Realisation

The most important leitmotif of western academic work on China in the 1980s and 1990s was that dismantling collective agriculture, rural healthcare and education, privatisation and decentralisation of these activities, and the nearly rule-free activities of foreign enterprises in China were all to the unalloyed good of China and its people. The leadership, specifically at the provincial and lower levels in China collaborated in this enterprise of privatisation and decentralisation because they benefited from it by the accumulation of personal wealth and power. We will examine this phenomenon in some detail later, in Chapter IX. However, a brief summary here would be useful. When land was sold for industries and construction, Party cadres, who had inside knowledge of the plans, took part in the transactions and picked up assets. Cadre salaries were decided by the Party at various strata and were periodically hiked far beyond increase in the cost of living. Independent of their personal motives, the leadership also encouraged those who were keen to and capable of selling this line to the wider world. That too was quite natural. For the western scholarship that lives by 'publish or perish', it would be fatal to jeopardise the chance to get a visa to conduct field work in China. That is incentive enough to challenge the integrity of all but the most courageous. The remarkable fact is that there are so many who are so courageous among Western scholars and journalists who cover China.

The opening of China in the late 1970s was in many ways a restoration and resumption of the process that was initiated through the use of force by the West in the 19th century and interrupted by the Mao era and the experiment with social justice and equity carried out during that time. The work started in peace and respect for China by Matteo Ricci and his friends in the late 16th century and continued with disdain for China and violence towards it in the 19th century by the traders, like the opium selling Taipans, Jardine and Matheson, finally met with success – the work of converting China to western ways, along the secular path even if the religious route met a dead end. Most of China studies were done in this atmosphere of 'open door is good for China' and, by extension, for everybody else. Along with this came the argument that we were lagging in 'liberalisation' and, thus, 'falling behind' China.

Chapter VIII

India and China since 1949

At this juncture, it may be useful to take a pause and look at how we in India looked at China that was emerging from semi-colonial condition into freedom. We began this study by pointing out how little we knew each other as we became free at about the same time and we had a live border for the first time in history. In India, China was looked at as another Asian country liberating itself and reasserting its national spirit after the humiliation of external dominance for more than a century and a half, just as India too was doing, so that both would be good partners in independent development and in non-aligned international politics. The expectations of a trouble free future partnership was seen as accentuated by the presence of Mao, the Head of State in the Indian embassy reception in Beijing on January 26, 1951 to mark the first anniversary of Indian Republic. Overriding protocol that discourages Heads of States from attending such receptions in embassies, Mao even spoke on behalf of the Chinese government. He said, "Indian nation is a great nation and the Indian people are a great people" before proposing the customary toast to our President and the people of our country. The People's Republic's right to China's seat in the UN was first advocated by India in 1950, at the first opportunity after the establishment of the new government in China. This engagement culminated in India's active efforts to involve China in the non-alignment movement through the Bandung Conference and the agreement on Tibet in 1954.

Indian scholarship and even school curriculum reflected this benign approach. Historians wrote about China within the inclusive perspective of Asian resurgence. The finest example of this genre was K M Panikkar's magisterial *Asia and Western Dominance,* which sought to write for the first time, and perhaps the only time, a history of Asia since the arrival of Vasco da Gama at Kozhikode in 1497 through a freshly constructed Asian point of view that tried to integrate the experiences of the entire region from India to Japan. That a historian of Panikkar's stature and diplomatic experience thought that a composite Asian perspective overriding differing attitudes developed by many nations through thousand or more years of history could be identified and articulated was an eloquent illustration of the mood of the times in India. At the same time, such an approach obtained only in India among the countries studied by Panikkar. No such book was written in China, Japan, Korea, or Indonesia. Perhaps it was another example of the terrific impact of *The Discovery of India* and Nehru's vision for Asia on our historians writing not only on India, but other countries too.

School texts of the 50s too brought home to a generation of Indian children the story of colonial aggression on China including Japan's attack, the drama of the communist Long March, and the victory of Communism. Mao, Zhou Enlai, and Marshal Zhu De were familiar names. China was the only Asian country whose modern history was taught in our school when European history ruled the roost. A generation of Indians grew up with some knowledge about China and considerable goodwill towards it.

The 1962 War and Its Impact on China Studies

The entire edifice started getting undermined by 1958 with clashes at the border and China's blunt denial that any kind of agreed border existed between India and China, followed by an uprising in Tibet and the resulting flight of the Dalai Lama from Tibet. All this was quite a shock to the Indian public, who believed in age old friendship and brotherhood with China, peaceful coexistence and a common agenda that inspire both the countries. The entire thing collapsed with the invasion of India by China in 1962. Though this essay is intended to present an Indian point of view of China and not to examine India-China relations in detail, it is useful to look at how the 1962 war had consequences for China's image in India.

The war led to a virtual break in relations between India and China, as it was seen by the ordinary people of India as an unforgivable act of betrayal. This distrustful assessment still lingers even if in a milder form. China did not help matters in any way because it followed a policy of making hostile statements on virtually all that happened in India, calling the Indian government 'a reactionary clique' and 'expansionist'; and it steadily stepped up support and help for Pakistan including diplomatic aid on the Kashmir issue despite that country's alliance with the USA and much before Pakistan internationalised the Kashmir issue. CPI (M), which was seen to be pro-Chinese in India, was dubbed 'revisionist' by the Chinese. It was all part of the Chinese foreign policy at that time, which focused on confrontation with and subversion of states in its periphery.

Given the strong public reaction in India, it would have been impossible to maintain normal relations between India and China. The extreme positions taken by China ensured that business as usual was not possible, and gave the impression that it was, perhaps, not even wanted by the Chinese. The embassy in Beijing was without an ambassador; there was no trade; and there were no sports or cultural exchanges, which would not have been possible once the Cultural Revolution started. Even direct telephone communications were not possible for some time. All these were predictable between countries having substantial political difficulties, but what was worse was that all other pathways of communication were shut down too. The government prohibited the entry of Chinese publications, magazines and even newspapers and daily bulletins of the Xinhua News Agency. Access to materials needed to study China was possible only for scholars affiliated to the government run institutions and/or for those, who received a special dispensation from the authorities. How did this dispensation affect our capacity for high quality assessment on China based on our specific interests?

The closing of the windows and shutting out of the breezes on the fear that we would be swept off our feet by Chinese propaganda – to turn on its head the famous Tagore image on the inherent openness of India – and the defensive mentality that engendered it was one of the worst consequences of the 1962 war, far worse than the military and security impact it caused, because it lasted longer, was far more difficult to remedy and was deeper, being a psychological wound rather than a physical wound that heals easily and faster. Even before the shooting war, the Indian Finance Ministry had banned the entry of books, periodicals and other printed materials containing 'erroneous depiction' of Indian borders. At one point, that Ministry considered banning even the *Encyclopaedia Britannica*! Only when it dawned on them that it would only embarrass us in the eyes of the world, but do nothing to the Chinese that the Ministry relented and agreed to let all publications enter with offending maps blacked out. What happened was that our people were blacking out the map of our own country! Mao's writings, dealing exclusively with the theory of communism, got in only after a legal fight. The itch to ban, so against our culture, never disappeared totally. In this atmosphere of suspicion, absence of basic research materials and disappearance of professional opportunities outside the government, China as an academic subject for research withered in India. By the time it revived, the perspectives were so warped that it had become impossible to remedy.

Limitations of China Studies

There were two reasons for this. The first was that, thanks to the near monopoly that the government had over primary sources on China, there was a bias towards the study of precisely those aspects of China that were of interest to the government. The main subject was the border and the strength of the relative claims of the two sides. Indian scholarship on this subject is of high quality, demonstrating what a level of excellence our scholars can achieve in a field of their choice. However, our experts studied or wrote little on China's economy or its domestic situation on the basis of their own studies and from the perspective of India's interest, or how any of these issues had impact on China's India policy, if at all. Problems like population control, ethnic minorities, rural health care and education, extension work in agriculture, land reform, food security, water management, to name a few, ought to have been of common concern. After all, is there another country for India to compare itself with other than China and vice versa when it comes to experience in coping with challenges of such a large mass of people, particularly in rural areas? Would it not have been useful to compare the effectiveness of the strategies of both the countries in these spheres? China's land reform was effective, but very violently carried out; but there was much to learn from its experiments in food security, water management and rural health care, which, we have already seen, produced superior social indicators. What kinds of studies were made in these areas in the '60s and '70s by us to discover anything of use to us? The haze of goodwill dulled our faculties in the '50s and the closing of our mental doors later led to a failure of proper comprehension and critical interpretation that could have benefited us.

Foreign Expertise Fills the Vacuum

Thanks to this indifference, the field was left wide open for foreign expertise to enter with its agenda. Western expertise was developed from its own critical point of view and was used by these countries to promote their ideological agenda of influencing the Chinese to validate their agenda for them. Historically, China was admired in the West as a sophisticated and elegant civilisation with much to teach the West, in contrast to the condescending attitude it displayed towards India, the Arabs, or even Russia. Mateo Ricci's introduction of Confucius as the wisest of philosophers was the first step in this process. The anti-clerical French thinkers of the 18th century, who proved to be of great influence in later European thought, admired Confucius as progressive and modern precisely because he too ignored religion and studied the way to social harmony. The sheer duration of China's civilisation was seen as another plus. Though its unchanging nature repelled many thinkers like Adam Smith, Hegel and Marx as irremediably backward, to others, it was the ultimate in social cohesion exemplified in the statement, much echoed, that "China is the only empire which has solved the social question for an extended period, the only one in which the mass of the population was ever happy."[14] As we have seen, it was the largest mass of people on earth ripe for conversion for the Missionary and ready as a market for the Merchant. China beckoned everybody; in the West, it was also sold by everybody.

It goes without saying that contacts with China in the field of academic studies have been revived and have been expanding since political relations between India and China began to thaw since 1976 and after China opened for such exchanges since the 1980s. This will not be the place to review, somewhat, the status and content of China studies in India, except to state that academic institutions have established mechanisms for better interaction. It is to be hoped that when the BRICS group develops and India takes part in the Shanghai Cooperation Organisation, there will be a fillip to China studies on a far larger range of subjects that would be of practical benefit to India.

Chapter IX

Chinese Economy and Society in the 'Open' Era

The closing down of the agricultural communes that were set up in the late '50s was the most important move in China's opening. When communes were formed, all land, except a small plot on which the individual peasant could grow vegetables and rear animals, came under the ownership of the commune along with agricultural implements. Produce net of seed, fodder and a fixed quantity for local consumption, usually 13-15 kg per person per month, was levied by the government for the distribution of grains in the cities.[15] All other items of use by the members of the commune and any additional requirement of grain had to be bought with work points earned by individual members in proportion to the work put in. This measure effectively made grain the currency. Further, the farmers lost their power over the decision on what to plant, because that became part of the national plan and came by the fiat of Party cadres. The closing down of such a system should not excite us in India as a great act of liberalisation in which China went ahead of India because, in India, agriculture has always been not only private, but tax free. We should also remember that the sale of land in open market is still not possible in China and title to land is hemmed in with severe restrictions. Therefore, the frequently made claim that China liberalised ten years earlier than India is baseless. Collectivisation of land also has quite a pedigree in China, even in imperial days. The old governments of imperial times were also monopoly traders in silk, tea, salt etc. and maintained long standing procedures for buying rural produce and distributing it to stabilise prices. Therefore, collective tilling of land was not so dramatic a departure from the past; but loosening that arrangement was a break with the tradition, which brought agriculture on par with the practice of capitalist economies. When the communes were disbanded, agricultural production rose steeply and contributed significantly to the increase of economic growth rates.

Breakdown of the Welfare State and Flight from Villages to Cities

What is less known to us is how the welfare measures of Mao's first decade were also dismantled step by step at that time. Peasants had, then, to pay a variety of taxes including for housing, rent for the land cultivated, fees for medical treatment and schooling of children, thus terminating the social protection offered to them since Liberation. In an essay entitled 'The Crisis in the Countryside',[16] Li Changping, an experienced rural cadre described the conditions at the turn of the millennium in his village in the fertile Hubei province through which flows the great Yangzi River. He noted that an average farmer earned a net income of 3600 yuan from which he had to a pay a capitation tax based on the size of his family, rent for his agricultural plot, tax on housing, school fees, costs for medical care and any other tax that the local party chooses to impose, in addition to being dragooned for free labour in irrigation and flood control works, etc. As the peasant had to spend 600 yuan per annum to put a child through primary school and double the amount for the secondary school, Li Changping concluded that agriculture was a loss-making business for peasants. He noted that taxes increased because the Party and government bureaucracy kept becoming larger. When tax burden became unbearable, peasants fled their villages for larger cities. This suited the rulers of China because they had simultaneously opened the Exclusive

Economic Zones and needed labour at bargain rates to attract foreigners and overseas Chinese to make investments in them. Thus, the squeeze on the peasants was deliberately engineered so that local governments generated funds for their functioning, while a huge army of workers became available for the new factories being set up. China does not allow free travel of its people from one place to another. By administrative procedures since the establishment of the People's Republic, which were enacted as law in 1958, the population was divided into city dwellers (*jumin*) and village dwellers (*nongmin*) with inheritance of status through mother. Peasants became some kind of a hereditary caste as this law aimed to "tie the cultivators to the land, making sure that cheap labour was available in the collective farms from which a surplus was taken to pay for industrialization."[17] Transfer of residence will require permission from the place of original residence. As almost all the peasants had run away without such approval, they were without residential documents in the factory cities. The result was that they were liable to some taxes in the villages they escaped from, but were not eligible for entitlements in the cities, like medical care, subsidised housing and schooling for their children. Even now, the migrants live in jerry built multi-storey housing in Shenzhen, the earliest EEZ, where *The Economist* reported once that they rented eight sq. metres of space for $100 per month (That magazine was of the opinion that this was a very good deal!). They got squeezed from all sides while the government got the EEZs started without having to worry about welfare measures for the workers deployed there. Those, who wanted us to follow China with our own EEZs, had obviously not studied the methods used by the Chinese authorities to get them set up. In the Third Plenum of the 18th Party Congress held from November 11 to 15, 2013, a decision was taken to eliminate this system, which was estimated to benefit around 200 million people, who had migrated without approved procedures in the past several decades. At the same time, this was not an administrative or procedural problem that could be solved at the stroke of a pen. Cities had benefited thus far by denying city dweller benefits to all these people including the right to schooling for the children. Rural areas taxed them without having to offer them services. It would be a massive challenge for the urban areas to equalize benefits for such a vast number of people and for the rural administrations to sustain services while being deprived of substantial revenues.

The sheer number of migrants depressed the wages, which suited the investors. As they were not legal residents, they could not resort to any collective bargaining, another gesture by the Chinese Communist Party to their capitalist friends. Migration was seen as such an attractive business that the governments in densely populated but poor inland provinces even raised revenue by rounding up and sending people to coastal provinces for placement in factories. The lack of residence papers also opened up a fertile area for police corruption. Even in the first decade of the 21st century, the police was arresting about two million people every year, resulting in more than 700 custodial deaths. Such a vast range of violence and exploitation was tolerated for the benefits of business, mostly foreign enterprises, only because of the total absence of rights for the people.

Thus, the change in regulations in both agriculture and industry created a huge class of people who could be squeezed fully to produce goods for exports at the lowest costs. It is, therefore, not surprising that the World Bank concluded in a study made in 1990 that 6.4 percent of the annual growth of nine percent came from increased investment, 2.1 percent from increase in labour force and only the marginal remainder from technical upgrading. The Labour Law enacted in 1994 fixed a 44 hour work-week with no more than 36 hours of overtime per week. The only way migrant labour could survive in the discriminatory conditions was by working the maximum possible hours of overtime. Factories supplying international markets also set up illegal factories, which did not exist officially and, thus, did not pay overtime. That is why the eminent economist Hu Angang concluded, "It is the constant and continued sacrifice of the excluded majority in the Chinese villages that makes the Chinese economic miracle possible" because "the peasantry .... lacks a voice of its own in the society, having neither real political representation in the decision making process nor institutional channels to affect policy making."[18] Thus, we see that, while they were used to extract surpluses for industrialisation in the earlier days of the People's Republic, the peasants are now used more directly for the same purpose, but once again, by severely circumscribing their rights. The other side of this equation is that, in the absence of significant technical upgrading and productivity increase, any reduction in the constant supply of fresh labour is bound to have an adverse effect on growth.

That this was not a temporary arrangement to tide over a critical period, but an ingrained mindset of the power elite can be deduced from the comment made as recently as 2007 by the Deputy Chair of the Legal Committee of the National People's Congress explaining the revised regulations for investors, "If there is some bias in the application of the law, it would be in favour of the foreign investors because local governments have great tolerance for foreign investors to attract and retain investment."[19] We can all decide for ourselves whether such a statement would be made in public by any responsible politician in India and, if somebody chooses to do so, how long he or she will survive in the job. Learning from China is more complicated than one imagines.

Workers No Longer the Leading Class

What happened to industries was something parallel to the effect reform produced in villages. By 1956, China had completed the nationalisation of its economy and contractual labour disappeared as a result. The Chinese Constitution declared workers to be the leading class, making them 'masters of their production unit'. In practical terms, their wages were unilaterally set by the state with no opportunity for collective bargaining. The government also withheld approximately half their earnings for investment. This forced deprivation was partly compensated by the prestige workers enjoyed as the leading revolutionary class and, in more practical terms, by the offer of non-cash benefits like food, clothing, housing etc. at subsidised rates with lifetime guarantees and other welfare measures covering birth, education and healthcare for their families and even funeral arrangements. The social scientist Wen Tiejun summarised this arrangement as the appropriation of the bulk of the surplus produced by the workers at very low cost in return for a guarantee of lifelong security and promise of a better future, popularly known in China as the 'iron rice bowl', which would always be there and cannot be broken.

What happened in the '80s was a comprehensive violation of this solemn compact with the people. Quoting Wen Tiejun's observation cited above, Wang Yi of Chengdu University concluded, "Starting from the mid-80s when a full fledged labour contract reform was launched .... A process of betrayal set in. The obligation of the government under the previous system was never converted into any form of contractual labour relations. The state had no intention of reflecting in cash terms its own obligations. On the contrary, it has continuously sought to evade under the cover of 'legalisation' the historical responsibility voluntarily assumed on the very first day the Chinese Communist Party raised its revolutionary banner."[20] Thus was the 'iron rice bowl' broken as a result of the much extolled liberalisation. An illustration of this process can be seen from the way workers' housing was dealt with. When state owned firms were asked to raise their own funds, they cancelled the housing arrangements, in effect expropriating what the workers had acquired through their labour as return for the savings they had made for investment and national development. They had to save all over again to buy the housing which, in fairness, was their right from the beginning. Even this was not the end. City Administrations routinely ordered people out and took over properties in attractive locations for redevelopment and pushed the owners to more distant suburbs. Compensation was inadequate; there were no means of public agitation or legal redress. In most cases, the land taken over thus was sold to developers in sweetheart deals without auction or any similar transparent procedure. Most of the millionaires in China amassed their wealth through such arrangements with the ruling party.

How Beijing and Shanghai Grew Vertically

For example, half a million families were evicted from Beijing between 1991 and 2003 by developers who had acquired the right to build in that land. Most of the land was in the historic parts of the city with lanes called hutungs, full of houses with courtyards that lent some charm to an otherwise drab city. In most places, they would be preserved as heritage sites. Most of them were expropriated to build high rises and office buildings. "It took twenty-eight days to demolish the houses of 2100 families .... We finished the demolition and relocation work on the streets and it caused a sensation in Beijing. There were no appeals. No negative reactions at all!"[21] boasted a Party official turned private developer about one such action. Naturally! If the government officials turn themselves into businessmen and lead the work, if there are no courts and elected bodies to protect individual rights and there is no free press to debate the matter, there will be no negative reaction, but only arbitrary action. As compensation was unilaterally fixed, it is estimated that the owners lost at least seven billion Yuan (in the range of Rs. 4000 crores) and the city lost 5.5 billion Yuan by not using market rates for sales. This destruction of historic neighbourhoods has been replicated in all the cities of China in the name of development. When we remember that China is the oldest of settled countries and had large cities for an extremely long time with an enormous number of historic neighbourhoods, it would be fair to conclude that the loss of tradition has been more massive than anywhere. Now we know how the high-rises that everybody gapes at in awe came into being.

Shanghai deserves special attention in this context because it is held up as the absolute example of the city of the future. Those contemplating its skyline, especially those from India, wax eloquent about it. Three thousand buildings of more than 18 storeys built since the 1990s. There is something deeply unhealthy about this infatuation of foreigners with Shanghai, particularly the Indian obsession with tall buildings abroad. What is forgotten is that Shanghai was developed almost entirely by the government and that investment in Shanghai has been the most blatant example of the anti-rural and pro-urban bias of the reform era in China. More than a million people were shifted out to make way for the high-rises. The Shanghai Formula One track ate up $ 1 billion in public funds, surely an indication of extravagance and corruption, as a very good track was built in India for Rs. 300 crore by private parties. So also with the tennis complex that swallowed $ 300 million. The much touted maglev that connects the city and its airport is so expensive that it would not recoup the investment for 160 years. Shanghai has fewer private enterprises than any part of China, except the national capital and Tibet. Quite appropriately, it was defined by Milton Friedman, who understood free markets more than anyone else as 'a statist monument to a dead pharaoh on the level of the pyramids', the then dead pharaoh being Deng Xiaoping. Is it the same city about which a scholar steeped in humane traditions like Dr. Manmohan Singh said later, "I do believe that Mumbai can learn from Shanghai's experience in reinventing itself, rebuilding itself, in rediscovering itself." Which speechwriter misled him into saying that the city that is the cradle of our free enterprise, the city where our autonomous industry was born, the city that should be our Manhattan, has to learn from the place called 'a statist monument' by Friedman much earlier? This too illustrates the extent to which standard lines on China propagated by a particular type of scholarship infects the thinking in India.

The pattern of seizure of land without adequate compensation, secret deals between Party leaders and real estate developers for mutual enrichment, and expulsion of residents to far suburbs are enacted in city after city. One result is that housing has become unaffordable, a potential source of widespread unrest. The Nobel Prize winner, Mo Yan said recently that he would use the prize money of ten million Swedish Krona to buy a house in Beijing – given his characteristic tongue in cheek and ironic style, a devastating comment on housing conditions in the capital of the country.

Obviously, somebody gained from this exploitation of surplus rural labour and the deprivation of wages of labour inflicted upon the working class. It was the coalition of the Party cadre and the foreign entrepreneur; the go between in this corrupt liaison was the overseas Chinese businessman.

The Role of Hong Kong, Retained as a Self-governing Colony, in this Growth Story

The foundation for this corrupt liaison was laid with the EEZs. Was it a coincidence that the first set of ports to be opened as EEZs in the 1980s was precisely the same group that was opened by force by the Western invaders in the 19th century in the first violation of Chinese sovereignty by the Europeans and the USA? It can hardly be. The money for the EEZs came first from Hong Kong, a foreign enclave of China carefully preserved by China for its uses. This was followed by letting Taiwan in, no matter all the rhetoric about it being run by a 'bandit clique' and its people waiting to be liberated by the communists. Here was another signal that China has taken a big turn away from past policies so that colonies are preserved and fostered and rebel provinces greeted politely for the sake of the investment they bring. Hong Kong was also useful as the Headquarters of companies claiming to be Chinese, but free of the restraints of China's regulations, because it also provided facilities of a world class financial centre, the benefits of free enterprise with transparent regulations, rule of law, freedom from corruption, none of which would be available in China. For example, Lenovo, which was set up after IBM sold a part of its business, is called a Chinese company, but it is a Hong Kong company set up under the Foreign Equity Law, which allows substantial tax incentives on FDI that is not available to domestic firms. One consequence of the use of Hong Kong for setting up companies free of Chinese regulations is that the money taken out of China illegally comes back as FDI in what is called 'round-tripping', which puts under question the data about huge FDI that China attracts year after year. Hong Kong has relatively free political atmosphere, legal existence as a separate customs entity with a voice and vote in the WTO, and an autonomous administration with its own Constitution. China tolerates them only because open financial arrangements of Hong Kong are vital for China and they would not at all work without all the legal protections provided by the rule of law and reasonably free political atmosphere including protection of free speech. It is also notable that despite all the investments there for over more than three decades, Shanghai has not come anywhere near Hong Kong as an internationally important financial centre, again for the simple reason that the legal and political situation there does not help foster the same business climate.

We will have a closer look at the role of FDI in the China growth story. We will only note here that Hong Kong played a crucial role, not only in the earlier days of socialist control, but also in the days of opening of China. $ 41 billion out of $ 92.4 billion of FDI in 2008 came from Hong Kong. A separate and more or less independent Hong Kong has been indispensable for China to develop and grow.

This situation is unique to China and cannot be replicated, thus making the entire question of China being a model for other developing countries quite irrelevant. Even if EEZs and other forms of encouraging FDIs are created, it will be impossible for any other country, certainly India, to create a Hong Kong by ceding a part of its territory with different laws and a different political regime.

The Uses of Taiwan

The case of Taiwan too is quite interesting. After the establishment of the People's Republic in 1949, the defeated armies of Chiang Kaishek landed in Taiwan and continued to rule there claiming to represent the entire China. They also held China's seat in the UN with the support of the USA and most of the countries of Europe and Latin America. China all along considered the regime to be a rebel entity. They insisted that the countries wishing to establish relations with them should recognise Taiwan as a part of China.

After China and the USA resumed contact at Warsaw in 1969, there was a gradual change in China's position in the world. As we have seen earlier, barely 50 countries had embassies in Beijing in the '60s. In 1970, Canada established diplomatic relations with China when China accepted a formulation through which Canada 'took note of' China's position on Taiwan rather than explicitly accepting it. This 'adjustment' of China's stand was a useful precedent that helped a large number of other countries to follow the Canadian formula and start relations with China. This arrangement allowed all the countries to keep some kind of a quasi-embassy in Taiwan while having a proper embassy in Beijing.

When Nixon arrived in Beijing, China started the negotiations with that important holdout by demanding that the USA break all relations with Taiwan before they proceed with any kind of negotiations. But they quickly came down and settled for a variation of what they had agreed with Canada on the status of Taiwan. They even accepted that the USA could open a liaison office in Beijing while the Americans retained their embassy in Taiwan and continued to protect it with a defense agreement and regular supply of weapons. This shows how much China had climbed down to obtain diplomatic recognition from the USA and to have an accommodation with it in the face of the threat from the Soviet Union. The USA waited for another seven years before recognising the People's Republic while retaining military relations with Taiwan and ensuring that China could not attack the rebel province.

The accommodation with the USA allowed China to open its EEZs for investment by Taiwan and the tapping of its considerable technological knowhow. Taiwan is very rich and has a range of high tech industries. Opening of China to Taiwan helped China upgrade its production, improve the technical skills of its workforce, and widen its industrial capacity as the Taiwanese set up factories and trained the workers. The relations expanded to include tourism, preferential trade and other paraphernalia of normal relations between any two countries.

Taiwan became a functioning democracy after Chiang Kai-shek and his son and successor passed away in quick succession. The Party in opposition to Chiang's Guomindang campaigned on a platform of independence. Their victory in the presidential election annoyed China, but they did not wish to do anything that would disrupt trade and investment. The Chinese Parliament adopted an Act, which promised the use of force in case Taiwan declared independence. Though it appeared to be an aggressive posture, it was, in fact, a strong signal that as long as Taiwan does not do anything precipitate like declaring itself to be a separate country, the current de facto independence of Taiwan will be accepted and the two governments will coexist. Taiwan has no urgent reason to declare independence because it is so for all practical purposes with liaison offices that function as embassies in most countries, membership in WTO and the Olympic movement, etc. Except for membership in the UN, Taiwan has all the attributes of a sovereign nation. Investment, technical knowhow and contact with businessmen from Taiwan are far too important for China to start a conflict. China cannot also afford the ill-will that a war will generate. Thus, China benefits from the status quo on Taiwan and its existence as a separate economic entity with political freedoms as it does with Hong Kong.

The Role of FDI in China's Growth

Thus, China became capitalist because of foreign capital and not because it produced and nurtured a domestic capitalist class that was independent of the ruling class, an entrepreneurial culture, rule-bound financial and investment climate and transparent legal procedures. By now, China has also had the experience of capitalist system for longer than socialist planning. Capitalism with Chinese characteristics developed on the foundations of the FDI. As we saw earlier, the old treaty ports were opened as EEZs. This was followed by the planned construction of Shanghai as a base for foreign entities. China grew at around eight percent for the three decades after its opening (It is not true that the growth rate was invariably above eight percent or more. Chinese have gone on record that growth was much lower in many years in the 1990s. China growing at nine percent or more for more than 30 years without break is just a journalistic flourish. It is also a truth universally accepted that China adjusts its data on annual growth to make its growth smooth and even). This is also not that unusual. Taiwan had ten percent growth rate for more than two decades. Japan grew at eight percent through the '60s and '70s. South Korea also did so for almost 30 years till the Asian financial crisis hit it in 1997. Still, China is much larger and its growth at a significant rate had a beneficial impact on much larger number of people.

Equally relevant is the data that between 1978 and 2004, the estimated FDI in China was $ 560 billion. For the shorter period of 2005-2011, the total FDI was a monumental $ 585 billion, far more than what was invested in China in the previous 20 years. What China used was more than twenty times what Japan received between 1945 and 2000 so that China reached near the level of Japan's GNP. Even if we adjust for the value of the US dollar, it is clear that China has used FDIs far more inefficiently than Japan. In the early 21st century, China achieved growth rates historically attained by Japan with one-third extra investment and double of what Taiwan and South Korea managed with. China was inefficient in the use of capital and failed to achieve the same level of productivity increases and technological upgrading or both compared to Japan, Korea and Taiwan. The only other possibility is that a large part of the money was being siphoned off. As an aside, we can also ask the question that is seldom asked, why we in India with its much lamented low level of FDI grew at the rate of at least 80 percent of China year after year, at least till a few years back. We have already seen how growth in China is based almost entirely on investment and labour. What if one or both taper off?[22]

Aid Received by China

In the midst of all the hype about China, the subject of development assistance received by that country is brushed under the carpet.

Since 'liberalisation', China received around US $ 2 billion per annum on an average as development assistance, or soft loans and grants, in the beginning, going up to $ 3.5 billion in 1995 and slowly tapering off to $ 1.5 billion by 2008. The biggest source of official development assistance (ODA) is Japan, a country the Chinese love to hate. When China and Japan established diplomatic relations and signed the peace treaty that terminated the state of war existing between the two countries, China waived war reparations, but ensured that Japan actually paid them in the guise of ODA beginning from 1979. Till 2008, Japan had offered Yen 3.1331 trillion as loans, Yen 145.7 billion in grants, and Yen 144.6 billion as contribution to technical cooperation activities. Why Japan provides aid to a country that boasts of a foreign exchange reserve of $ 2 trillion and claimed at that time to be approaching Japan in GNP, one can only say that the Japanese public too is asking the same question. The modern airports in Beijing and Shanghai are Japanese aid projects as is the Beijing metro. Chinese would, of course, not mention this. Japanese aid was also used to build ports at Shenzhen, Qinhuangdao and Dalian, several railway lines, power stations, sewage systems, hospitals, afforestation projects, tuberculosis control program, and for upgrading the Baoshan steel mill. As comparison, let us note that India, which was the first country to which Japan extended ODA, became the largest recipient of ODA from Japan overtaking China only by 2011.

Foreign Trade and GDP Data

A few years back, it was announced that China was overtaking Japan and becoming the second largest economy. Hardly anybody clarified that this calculation was on the basis of the concept of purchasing power parity, which is not an entirely reliable measure of the prosperity of a country. The excitement about China overtaking Japan and catching up with the USA should wait.

The second point for us to note is about trade. Without cluttering up this essay with a lot of tables, it can be stated that there are some interesting features about China's trade. If we compare

China's total trade surplus and the surplus with the USA, it will be seen that they are almost the same year after year or that China's trade surplus with the USA is larger than its total trade surplus. Readers interested in details that prove this conclusion could look at the data given in the notes.[23] In other words, it can be said that China has a balanced trade relationship or runs a small deficit in trade with the countries other than the USA. If, China's exports to countries other than the USA suffer, as is happening with the EU area during the past few years because of the European economic crisis, China's export machine is in trouble.

The third point is that all the money China earns as surplus from its export to the US goes back to the US. China has kept most of its trade surplus in US Treasury securities, which fund the budget deficits that the US has regularly run. This is described unnecessarily dramatically as the Americans going hat in hand to China. This is not true because there is no compulsion that the Chinese should invest in the US Treasury notes. It is a conscious decision by their Central Bank and, all central banks being political entities, it is a conscious decision as the result of some unstated or tacit quid pro quo arrangement. A stable USA that keeps buying from China is obviously good for China. Offering money to troublesome outsiders to keep them at bay is also an age old Chinese tactic going all the way back to the powerful Han dynasty, which used to offer tons of gold annually to the marauders from Mongolian steppes.

Nobody doubts that China has grown significantly and that the living conditions of the people have improved noticeably. At the same time, many experts had reservations about the Chinese data, which were not too well expressed till recently. Finally, in 2013, major discrepancies were discovered in trade data, which could not be explained and the Chinese were compelled to promise that they would 'improve' their statistics. The Chinese have also done some strange things in the past without attracting similar notice. In 2004, they revised the GNP with an abrupt addition of Yuan 2.3 trillion or a 16.8 percent increase, which, they said, corrected a past undercounting of the services sector. Once again, in 2008, they discovered another missing Yuan 1.3 trillion, which was also added to the basis for counting future growth. After the recent revelations about dubious trade statistics, the Nobel Prize winning economist, Paul Krugman asked whether Chinese data is a form of science fiction. We will meet with other problems with Chinese data later. At present, we can just note these and wonder how reliable Chinese data has been all along.

We would also note in passing that the comparisons that are made between India and China are all not quite valid as the two countries use very different methods for computing GDP. Till one of our experts does a comparative study based on similar parameters, we should refrain from conclusions.

Chapter X

The Party in the 'Open' Era

We should remember that cadres of the Communist Party ran the country and had exclusive control over the running of not only the state but also decision making on all aspects of the economy. In the case of urban enterprises, we must remember that the communist government destroyed an independent middle class soon after taking over in 1949. Along with the disappearance of the middle class went much of what may be called the soft infrastructure of free society, – independent rule of law, free media that monitors the authorities, and other organs of check like an autonomous audit, regulators of the market etc. China opened up without reconstructing any of these attributes of a civil society, which, in any case, cannot be brought into being overnight by the fiat of the government. The 'hard infrastructure' of roads and ports are made much more easily than those of the soft variety, which demand the difficult task of nurturing human resources as well as cultivating a particular attitude of mind. So, what happened in the '80s with the opening of the economy?

With the freeing of agriculture after the closing of the communes, agricultural production shot up and there were surpluses in rural areas. The workshops and commercial units owned by the communes, which made and repaired agricultural implements, did small scale manufacturing like processed food, bricks, herbal medicines, etc. for nearby markets, became free to grow. This was not the result of a conscious decision by the Party when it decided to abolish communes but the result of the play of market forces and an expression of the enterprising nature of the Chinese people. These were the famous TVEs, the Town and Country Enterprises that were closely studied at that time. In the last days of the communes, they comprised nine percent of China's industrial output, but by 1994, this had shot up to 42 percent. Strangely, they vanished by 2000.[24] Part of the reason was the turn towards emphasis on central planning that occurred in the mid 1980s, which reduced resources available to these free units. What else ailed them? In the vacuum of independent professional management and high quality supervisory mechanism, the control of these entities fell into the hands of cadres. However, there were no independent checks on their conduct as would be the case in an open society. Parallel to this, urban enterprises also had cadres, not all of them professional managers, running them as free enterprises by default. They had a good time running many of them to the ground and simultaneously enriching themselves. Social critic He Qinglian points out how the thrust of Chinese reforms had been 'to gradually reallocate the possession of social resources' in 'a process of privatisation of juridically public assets by the power-holding stratum'.[24] Sun Liping is more direct. He says, "The elite cadres began to love the markets and soon understood how to turn the power they wielded into personal accumulation of wealth, beginning the process of recomposing themselves into a property holding class.[25]" He describes the process in which 'in each upheaval in the distribution of resources the existing power-holders never missed out' because of the selective permission for admission to universities and for studies abroad, openings for speculation in the experimental urban reforms in the mid 80s and concludes, "These were all links in a chain of ubiquitous capital accumulation by this group. If a middle class had difficulty emerging in China, it is partly because so many of the resources necessary for one have already been cornered." Even official publications of those days had analyses of how cadres made money by bankrupting companies they managed. The result was 'stealing enterprises', as it was described by the workers, who ended up bearing all the losses. The rural enterprises created 12 million jobs per year between 1985 and 1995. This was decentralisation and innovation at its best. Then the central government changed the procedure about tax collection to increase their revenues. This development was followed by the Asian financial crisis. These two combined to strangle the TVEs. The greed of the cadres did the rest.

Cadres increased their numbers and paid themselves higher wages. The government payroll increased from 20 million persons in 1990 to 46 million in 2004. This was obviously a plan to appease the discontent of the urban chattering classes after the upheaval of the Tiananmen, which was centred in urban areas and from where most of the cadres came. Critics of the government, members of the vigorous New Left whom we met earlier, estimated that 15 percent of GNP was being siphoned off through bribes, theft, and arbitrary and illegal charges collected at the local level from people. The arbitrary way in which the cadres could work is illustrated by the statistics that the government spent $ 13 billion in entertaining, enough to conduct four Olympics at the level of the Beijing Games. With the same gruesome logic, poverty line was lowered between 1998 and 2002 while wages of bureaucrats increased five times. This only demonstrates Francis Fukuyama's bleak conclusion that 'public servants are no different from any other economic agents in seeking to maximise their individual self interest.' This was an integral part of the urban bias and indifference to rural areas already noticed by us as characteristic of the Chinese government of that time. The government had to mollify the cities which revolted in 1989. Most cadres came from urban background because children of the peasantry no longer had the same competitiveness to rise in the party. By that time, the leadership of the Party was also of urban extraction and sympathy. The two leaders of the 1990s were engineers from Shanghai, Jiang Zemin and Zhu Rongji. This showed how the Party had changed from Mao's time.

Another illustration of the same point is the way sourcing of students to elite universities has changed since liberation. Beijing (पेयचिङ) University and Qinghua (छिङह्वा) University, also located in the capital, are the two universities that may be called the elites of Chinese institutions of higher studies. As graduates from the two universities would be recruited into the Party and the state machinery, the student population of the two universities could be compared to the higher civil service in India. In the '50s, about 50 percent of the students in the two universities had rural backgrounds, but it declined to 17 percent by 1999. Quite tellingly, there is no published data since then, though there is an estimate that barely one percent are of rural background at present. If the higher civil service in India is considered a comparable entity, the situation may be considered quite the reverse in our country. Such decay in the quality of rural schools is directly attributable to the government making schooling costly in villages so that dropouts increase and quality decreases. This is another illustration of the urban bias of the Chinese system. It can be sustained because the Party does not have to meet the judgment of the masses on a regular basis.

The Party Controls Everything

For all the claims about private enterprises and autonomy of businesses, the Party is all pervasive. It runs no less than 2800 ideology schools. It oversees think tanks, businesses, media, religious bodies, educational institutions, NGOs, companies, and even courts. Walmart stores have Party units. The Party has total control over personnel deployment in public sector. The key person for this purpose is the head of the Organisation Department of the Party, who has ultimate control over personnel files. That individual is always a member of the Standing Committee of the Party Politburo and, in many cases, goes much higher. Deng Xiaoping did that job, as did Hu Yaobang and Zeng Qiling, who was the mentor of President Jiang Zemin.

Now that the Communist Party has little to do with communism, it falls back on nationalist gestures. One example is the way the Great Wall, once a symbol of oppression, is now promoted by the Party as the best symbol of China's greatness. In 1984, Deng Xiaoping made the connection explicit with the slogan, 'Love China: Build the Great Wall'. So also with Confucius, who was attacked by all earlier communists as well as every single modernizing force as the abiding symbol of China's backwardness, but was resurrected as the sage in whose name the communist government runs institutes abroad. The Party has harked back to all the possible nationalist and Han chauvinist symbols without fail and fanned xenophobia without missing a single chance, whether it was the incident with the US aircraft brought down in Hainan or the collision between Chinese and Japanese ships.

How Did the Party Lose People's Trust?

In the 1980s, the cadres cornered the benefits from the loosening of Party and government control over enterprises and went on to live ostentatious lives quite at variance with the traditional principle of 'Serve the People' articulated by Mao and seriously implemented in the '50s. Family members of Party leaders established monopolies over selected industries over which the government loosened control. It happened with Deng Xiaoping and Li Peng, who was Premier during the crackdown of the Tiananmen incident. Allegations have been made that the recently retired Premier Wen Jiabao's family has a major stake in diamond trade. One can imagine how cadres at lower levels behave because they are not under the same kind of glare of attention as those at the centre.

It is notable that only the children of Party leaders, who study abroad, return in large numbers on the conclusion of studies. It is estimated that, of all Chinese who have gone abroad since such arrangements became possible, about half were from old families of intellectuals, who faced persecution during Mao's time and the rest split equally between those of rural backgrounds and children of cadres. The last group has a vested interest in coming back as they have the inner track to power on return. Though this writer is not aware of any similar study on Indian students, anecdotal evidence suggests that the situation is different, that children of officials stay on in places like the USA while those from private business families return. Mao foresaw this trend of looking for benefit from 'connections' and warned, "The children of our cadre are a cause of discouragement. They lack experience of life and society, yet their airs are considerable and they have a great sense of superiority. They have to be educated not to rely on their parents or martyrs of the past, but entirely on themselves," a piece of advice that may be germane to us in India too.

Some of the other causes of disaffection have been population policy, pollution and income inequality. All these need detailed treatment because they have impact on the entire country, implications for China's image, and for what they reveal about the party's decision making methods and its attitude towards those whom it governs.

Population Control and One Child Norm

China was always a very heavily populated country. As a tightly governed country, there have always been censuses even as far back as the Han times. There was a census in the Tang times that counted the subjects of the emperor as numbering 52,880,488.[26] Some undercounting would have been inevitable and the number could well be around 60 million. The sheer size of the country also ensured that invaders just dissolved in the Han mass, leaving not a rack behind. China was able to successfully carry out the policy of 'if you cannot beat them, make them join us' when it came to invaders only because of the size of its population. Despite the periodic famines, earthquakes that killed hundreds of thousands, regular bouts of anarchy at the end of dynasties, and the usual banes of the poor like flood and drought, China had 580 million people in 1954. At the same time, there were about 104 boys to 100 girls – quite consistent with the ways of nature. What was China's population policy at that time? Mao, who was the ultimate decision maker on this as on all other things, was ambivalent. While he complained that the production of children was the only thing not planned in China, he also felt that birth control was a form of silent genocide. Ultimately, he ended up opposing all forms of birth control. He wrote with much pride about socialist countries surviving a nuclear war because China was too populous to be destroyed totally. He compared the post nuclear war situation to a clean sheet of paper in which the most beautiful characters could be written. He also made the same arguments to Nehru, who was deeply shocked by Mao's indifference to the vastness of the calamity that he was calmly analysing.

Famine of 1959-61

What happened soon after was a practical demonstration of such thinking. The Great Leap Forward was launched with much fanfare, with sharp increase in food production as one of its objectives. Inevitably, as every village reported bumper harvest that was expected of them, they were asked to send the alleged surpluses to cities. As the data was fictitious, village cadres were in a fix; but they had no option except to send whatever they had harvested, leaving the people hungry first, then in the grip of famine. This situation was either withheld from the central leadership or they decided to ignore what was happening. Still, it is astonishing and hard to believe that the leaders of a tightly governed country like China were completely unaware of what was going on all over the country for more than a year. Either way, the result was the same. While famine gripped the whole of rural China, the official press printed pictures of wheat growing so thick that children could sit on the plants without crushing the stalks! Mao even went back to his ancestral village of Shaoshan in Hunan province after a gap of more than 34 years and wrote quite a beautiful poem about how 'in the evening mist the heroes come home', referring to the peasants, who were actually beginning to die in large numbers. President Liu Shaoqi, also from Hunan, had received troubling reports about the bad situation and went to his village where he had to do some real digging to get at the truth that people were surviving on the bark of trees and grass. Only this visit by the President brought the levying of grains to an end, but that did not end the rural misery.

It is remarkable that this vast calamity went entirely unreported at that time. Partly, it was due to the tremendous ability of the Chinese government to control news, especially bad news. They put it out that there were temporary problems because of adverse weather over the entire country, a stand repeated even today about that time. It only shows that even Chinese weather reports were not to be trusted as there was no natural calamity at that time. Despite political difficulties between the two governments, the USA offered food aid, which was duly rejected by China with the huffy statement that the Chinese people would overcome their challenges by themselves. At the same time, it is also an illustration of the willingness of the world to think the best of China, cut them a very large slack, that no serious investigation was undertaken by anybody.

The first time the true picture of what transpired came out when American demographers analysed population data released in the late 1980s and estimated that there were at least 30 million 'premature deaths' between 1956 and 1961.[27] Later, a few courageous Chinese investigators, especially a remarkable man named Yang Jisheng tracked the data from village to village over a twenty year period to compile a detailed record of famine deaths that he estimated at 36 million in a book titled *Mubei (Wooden Tombstone)* to bring out the truth including horror stories about widespread cannibalism during those years. In their comprehensively researched books, *Hungry Ghosts* and *Maos' Great Famine,* respectively by Jasper Becker and Frank Dikotter, the two authors convincingly demonstrated that the famine deaths were no less that 45 million people. They also pointed to a secret study ordered by Zhao Ziyang, who became Deng Xiaoping's right hand man before being removed from power and confined to house arrest in the aftermath of the Tiananmen uprising in June

1989, which revealed deaths ranging from 43 to 46 million. A government fell in our country because of the feckless policy of sterilisation that was carried out in some parts of the country. Here is the only country that is larger than ours where at least 40 million people, and probably 50 million people – between seven and nine percent of the population, the majority of whom were women and children – died over a three year period, and that too without anybody outside the country and quite a few within being aware of what was going on, thanks to the wrong-headed policy followed with utter indifference by the government – surely a crime against humanity by any definition. By comparison, the Soviet Union lost ten percent of its population during the Second World War fighting an enemy bent upon destroying their country – a heroic sacrifice. For what were the 40 to 50 million Chinese sacrificed? Why is this event absent from the consciousness of the world that now agonises over famines in some country or the other?

This terrible event was preceded by the death of nearly a million people in the political campaigns of the '50s and followed by the death of at least 15 million people, who were killed in the violence of the Cultural Revolution. It is a cruel thing to say and this writer says it with extreme reluctance; but, if one wipes out about ten percent of the population in less than ten years, and that too women and children, that would surely lay a good foundation for slow population growth in later years. We hear much about India having a larger population than China at some point in future and about China's 'success' in dealing with the population problem, but there is no discussion of how the Chinese government helped the process along. After reading this, are we as embarrassed about not doing so well, as we could have been before reading these four paragraphs?

Population and Rocket Science

The government was still not done with population control in China. With Deng Xiaoping came the one child policy. How was such a drastic policy formulated, debated and implemented?

The most amazing thing is that the policy paper in this case was written, not by social scientists and demographers, but by a nuclear scientist called Song Jian, who wrote down various projections of population sizes using equations for the calculation of missile trajectories and refined it with the help of systems analysis experts. He proved, as a result, that a one child norm would limit the population to one billion by 2000 and reduce to 700 million by 2050. The policy proposal was never debated by the National People's Congress, the Parliament of China, never drafted as the law of the land, and never tested for compliance with the Constitution, thus making its implementation illegal by any normal definition. The social and cultural implications of the policy were never debated before its promulgation. It was adopted by the Party as a policy and punishments for violations were also announced only by Party diktat.

The Party set targets for each area, established quotas for abortion, threatened women who refused to have them and used absolutely illegal methods of coercion to get what they wanted. Pressure was put on reluctant persons through fellow workers and family members, by demolishing their houses as punishment and sending entire families to jail. A huge 450,000 strong bureaucracy was created to run this mindless program. As always happens with a bureaucratic setup, once it is created, it is hard to close down; it starts lobbying to maintain and strengthen itself and becomes an independent pressure group. This happened with the abortion bureaucracy too. Given the bias for boys, sex determination tests are rampant along with selective abortion of female foetuses. The sex ratio that was quite normal in the 1950s has become so skewed that now there are 118 boys for hundred girls, making it one extremely large Haryana without Haryana's option of getting brides from elsewhere. By 2009, there were 37 million more males than females in China. For a country with such good social indicators, China is the only country where more infant girls die than boys. As with migrants, this too is a fertile field for corruption because cadres can look the other way and let favoured persons have more than one child. It is estimated that 80 million people live without being registered. Over and above, more than 150,000 children, almost all of them girls, are abandoned annually. After all, if girl babies are abandoned, one could try to have a boy and be compliant with the one child rule. Finally, there is the loneliness of the pampered single child and the psychological effects of such bringing up have been studied in detail.

What was worse was that rocket science did not work when it came to production of babies. The one billion target for year 2000 was overshot by a big margin. Target for stabilisation was reset for 1.1 billion, then at 1.25 billion but reached 1.34 billion according to the 2011 census. At what level would China's population peak? The US Census Bureau estimates that it will do so at 1.4 billion by 2028. The Chinese estimate that it will be at 1.5 billion in 2033. What is clear is that rocket science was wrong and the projection of 700 million by 2050 a daydream. What can one say about the decision making that uses such projections without checking and debating and resorts to drastic action in pursuit of such policies? Let us also note that the government claims to have avoided 340 million births through its drastic program. The ironic thing is that international agitators, who 'demand' that India should explain the millions, who are not born, are obediently docile and silent on China. Finally, the 3rd Plenum of the Party Congress, meeting in November 2013 took a decision to wind up the one child policy. However, this decision is also hedged in with several qualifications, which make it unclear how the abortion bureaucracy will get dismantled. In any case, this will not make any immediate difference because there is no way the population balance between those working, the young and the old can be restored on a quick basis.

Was all the personal heartbreak, as when the badly made school buildings collapsed in the Sichuan earthquake killing thousands of single children, the use of violence and the immense expense on the hated abortion doctors (one foreign writer narrated his travel in a bus where an abortion doctor reluctantly confessed to her trade and justified it by saying 'zhongguo ren tai duole' – 'there are too many people in China' – only to have others in the bus mutter after she got down, 'Zhongguo ren tai huaile' – 'in China people have become very bad')[28] necessary at all? Prof. Amartya Sen had pointed out that the results achieved in China had been achieved in Kerala during the same timeframe without violence or any kind of extra measures, exclusively through enlightened dissemination of information (Even the forced sterilisation of the 1970s did not take place in Kerala). Action in China was not merely futile. When targets were set, there was pressure on cadres and the offer of incentives to report that they had achieved them, just as their predecessors reported bumper harvests in 1959, especially because promotions were also tied to performance. False reporting was naturally rampant. When it came to school enrolment, these lies were further compounded, doctoring education data. It follows that data on a range of items, like health care, literacy, school enrolment and infant mortality get falsified. When rural areas report infant mortality rates comparable to Finland and Singapore, one has to question not just that data, but ask what other data is of a similarly dubious quality. Thus, there is overwhelming evidence that data on school enrolment, child health parameters and even population cannot be considered entirely reliable.

The most important consequence of the one child policy has been the steep decline in the working age population. The 15-59 years population cohort peaked at 70.1 percent in 2010. The under 14 portion was 14 percent, down from 23 percent in 2000. This had led to occasional calls for review of the one child policy, but there had not been any indication from the new government that assumed office in 2013 that they were even ready for any kind of reconsideration. If births decline so precipitously as has happened in the last thirty years, from where are the Chinese going to get the future working population? Secondly, each single child will have to take care of four grandparents and probably other elderly relations too, as the Chinese live longer now. This makes such an onerous demand on the young that China had to pass a law in 2013 to make it a legal obligation for youngsters to visit the elders in the family and take care of them, with punishments spelt out for negligence. Imagine that this has to happen in a country where filial piety was the greatest of virtues; where people in the old days kept mourning on their birthdays to remember the mother's suffering on that day! There are tangible economic consequences in addition to the emotional issues. We have already seen how the surplus labour was the main driver of economic growth in the past three decades. This situation will come to an end by 2015. The only way the economy can grow after that is by technological upgradation. This route would also mean higher wages. The Chinese strategy so far has been to be the factory of the world where inexpensive labour is the main selling point. This cannot go on for long. Perhaps, the government recognizes the inescapable situation that may be why President Xi Jinping said soon after he took over that GNP is not everything and that China has to get used to lower growth.

As in other matters we have reviewed earlier, there is the road not taken. Even in 1980, the Total Fertility Rate (TFR) in China was only 2.3 percent, a shade above the replacement rate of 2.1 percent. A moderate non-coercive policy could very well have stabilised the population at around the present level without the violence of the current policy, while reducing the births gradually so that an abrupt shortage of working people does not occur. China will become old before it becomes rich. If it ends up with too many elderly people, when it does not have the societal means to take care of them, and the working population shrinks so rapidly that it harms growth, the one child policy will be the culprit. It will also be a telling refutation of the assiduously built up propaganda about China's unique farsightedness in policy formulation.

Environment and Development in China

Development through industrialisation has always been a polluting business. Britain went through this experience first and struggled for long against the fog and filthy air and the attendant health problems. Anybody who has read Dickens has vivid pictures of the terrors of the smoke-choked London. Today we have become more sensitive to global environment damage caused by such industrial practices. Let us look at what China, a large country with the highest rates of economic growth, has done in this field in the past several decades.

It is now well known that China has passed the USA as the largest atmospheric polluter, having achieved in the last few decades what the Americans took nearly two centuries to accomplish. Even on per capita basis, China's share is many times that of India. China defends its practice by arguing about the historic quantum of pollution from the developed countries in an opportunistic alliance with the developing countries. As the total amount of pollutants emitted from China has crossed the amount from the USA, this argument wears thin. China also has nothing in common with the concerns of the poor developing countries, not even with India with whom it gets clubbed in the devious strategy of the West. China has no ideological affinity with the developing world and has never taken any initiative in multilateral fora on their behalf. What is strange is that our government had chosen to ally itself with China, let the Chinese shoot from our shoulders, and divert attention from them by getting us to engage the developed countries, because we are in a different league altogether on atmospheric pollution, have historically had profound respect for the principle of conservation and have a vibrant civil society that scrutinises government policies vigilantly and critically.

It has been established beyond doubt that China is profligate in the use of energy. A study by the WEF a few years back concluded that China uses three times the global average in energy, four times as much as the USA and eight times that of Japan. Pan Yue, the then environment minister, cited this study and added, 'what is more embarrassing, three times the rate for India'.[29] When he sponsored a Green GDP report in 2006, which showed that pollution caused $ 64 billion worth of damage, it was shelved and the entire exercise abandoned. More recently, another study showed that life expectancy in northern China was four and a half years less than the south because of increase in air pollution.

'Fog and Filthy Air'

As we saw in the case of birth control, China missed targets in pollution control too. China announced in 2001 that coal production would double by 2020, but did so as early as 2007. Soon after, China passed the USA as the largest polluter. To mark this dubious achievement, it released a so called national strategy, which was only an outline of policy intentions without specific targets. It was a propaganda exercise to mollify critics within and abroad. Pollution from China falls as acid rain in neighbouring countries, stunting growth of trees in Japanese forests. It has even reached the American shores. It is now an international problem.

Most of air pollution is due to the use of coal. It is natural for China to use coal because it has the largest reserves of this mineral. We too do so as we have large coal reserves. China produces two-third of its energy from coal. The problem is that 24,000 of the 28,000 mines in China are small and ignore most of the regulations on environment and safety. They also produce one-third of the total and, thus, cannot be ignored. As most of them are privately run by people in cahoots with local authorities, supervision is so slack that they are some of the most dangerous places to work in what is a very hazardous industry. China mines 35 percent of the total global production of coal, but accounts for 80 percent of deaths in mines. As small mines are mostly located in the poorer interior of China, even women and children work in mines out of lack of alternatives and in violation of regulations. No wonder even official figures accept that there are between 5000 to 7000 deaths annually in coal mines since reforms started. Independent researchers have pieced together data from primary sources to arrive at the estimate that between 20,000 and 40,000 lives are lost annually. Death rates in mines are calculated on the basis of fatalities per million tonnes of production. Indian average is 0.4, China's is ten times ours, that of the USA one tenth of ours.

It is the use of coal that has produced calamitous levels of air pollution in China. All the top 20 most polluted cities in the world are in China. Beijing said that it held a 'Green Olympics' only by banning cars and closing factories for the duration of the Games. The filthy air was back soon. It is no longer possible to see the top of buildings in Beijing on any ordinary day thanks to the permanent fog. Chinese data on air pollution is not considered reliable and people turn to the information put out by the US Embassy from its air quality monitors. Acid rain falls in one-third of the country's area; and deserts are expanding at the rate of 3,000 sq. kms per year. While a WHO study in 2007 arrived at the conclusion that 4,50,000 deaths per annum are attributable to air pollution, but pressure from the Chinese government got it suppressed.[30] Compare it with the canard the same organisation spread about AIDS deaths in India, which were withdrawn only after much lobbying and persuasion by our government.

Water Woes

China has the fourth largest supply of renewable fresh water in the world after Brazil and Russia, just behind Canada, at 2,800 cubic kms (India is seventh with Indonesia and the USA between China and us). Thus, China has 40 percent more water than India and, therefore a higher per capita availability. At the same time, China grows 70 percent of its food from irrigated land. Enormous number of dams and reservoirs have been constructed for this purpose. There are around 3,400 reservoirs and 27 major dams. It is the only country still constructing major dams and relocating people in huge numbers. At least 10 million people were moved for constructing dams in the Mao era. This was dwarfed by the Three Gorges dam, one of the most massive dams in the world, which displaced 1.5 million people. This unprecedented project was carried out despite reservations on its ecological impact and safety questions, especially in the light of the collapse of the Banqiao dam in Hunan in 1975 killing hundreds of thousands – an incident that the government suppressed just as it did the starvation deaths of 1959-61.

As a result of the uncontrolled misuse of water in a manner similar to energy use, the water table in northern China has been falling by a metre per year. The withdrawal of water has been so extensive that the Yellow River, once 'China's Sorrow' because of its massive floods, is drying up. It failed to reach the sea for the first time in 1972. By the end of the last century, it had dried up before reaching the sea for 226 days per year. One third of its fish species have vanished. The river, which is the cradle of Chinese civilisation, had its wetlands, marshes and small streams till a few decades back. Now, water is pumped up from deeper and deeper levels for agriculture. Now, more than 100 cities are considered severely water short and more than 600 deemed water short.

The solution thought up is to shift water from Yangzi to the north, a vast project with unpredictable consequences. This project is undertaken not to aid agriculture, but to supply the cities of the plain in the north with water so that they can continue their uncontrolled growth. Unlike the debate in India, there is no involvement of the provinces from where the water will be drawn, no input from civil society, no judicial review. Just as with the one child policy, the effects will be known decades later. But, as we have learned when we examined the structure and characteristics of the Chinese state, the ideologically centralized system just does not allow anyone else to be a party to decision making.

Water pollution also has consequences beyond China's borders. Most of the East China Sea has become unfit for fishing thanks to the waste water pumped from the coastal provinces. Twenty-five percent of global mercury emission is from China, which has an impact on fisheries that is yet to be calculated.

Bad Earth

The destruction of forests abroad is another way China exports its problems. Logging has been banned in most of China, but this is at the expense of heavy destruction in South East Asia. Less well known is the alliance between Chinese logging companies and

Russian mafia in Siberia that wipes out large tracts of forests.

In all cases, protests by environmentalists usually lead to their arrest and imprisonment. Can the world afford to have China grow this way? Let us recall what Gandhiji wrote while he was living in South Africa about industrialization of Britain, warning us against taking the same path, "God forbid that India should ever take to industrialisation after the manner of the West The economic imperialism of a single tiny island kingdom is today keeping the world in chains. If an entire nation of 300 million took to similar economic exploitation, it would strip the world like locusts." It can be argued that we ignored Gandhiji in this respect, but his thought still lingers with us as a salutary warning. How powerful and relevant is this warning to the entire world can be understood as we see what has been done to their own people by the Chinese in the name of development. At the conclusion of a sympathetic study entitled *Adam Smith in Beijing*, Giovanni Arrighi could not but quote Gandhiji; nor could he escape the conclusion that 'by relying too heavily on energy-consuming Western path, China's rapid economic growth has not yet opened up for itself and the world an ecologically sustainable development path. This reliance does not just threaten to bring the economic miracle to a premature end … It is both a result and a cause of the widening cleavage between those, who have been in a position to appropriate the benefits of rapid economic growth and those who have to bear the costs.'[31] Philip P. Pan, who covered Beijing as a journalist, came to a similar conclusion expressed more bluntly that the Communist Party retained power while benefiting from 'the betrayal of its founding ideology, the logic-defying contortions that the propagandists used to explain its reversal, the blind calculus that holding on to power was an end that justified any means – it all bred a cynicism in Party ranks and access to the riches of a booming economy quickly warped the Party state'.[32] Now, we will study how such inequalities grew in China and how the ordinary people react to such a situation and the environmental decay that affects them severely.

Inequality and Dissent in the Open Era

Let us now see how the Communist Party betrayed the mandate of the people by actually promoting inequality as a deliberate policy in the Deng and post-Deng era. The basic cause of such inequality was the steady loss of agricultural land to build cities and EEZs. An estimate by the Land Bureau found that China was losing arable land by 0.5 percent per year and when population would cross 1.5 billion, arable land would be only 0.17 acre per capita. Lester Brown's projection was that China would lose half its arable land between 1980 and 2030. On the short term, this is exactly what the Party wants, while postponing the worry about the future because only such a pressure on land would create the stream of rural landless poor, who have to, perforce, migrate to cities, thus providing cheap labour for the factories that export; the arrangement that satisfied the regime, the foreign investors and consumers in rich countries getting inexpensive goods. That the 160 odd million migrants had no rights and that their children could not easily go to schools was a secondary concern. By year 2000, barely two decades after reforms were launched, disparities opened up so wide that rural disposable income was RMB 2253 per annum as against 6280 in urban areas. It was around this time, we have already seen, that the government lowered the poverty line and repeatedly increased the wages of cadres and bureaucrats. By 2009, the gap widened from 1: 2.8 to 1: 3.3 though incomes went up all around.

Money Laundering

Global Financial integrity has issued an estimate of the money taken illegally out of China in the decade ending 2009. Their estimate is that the developing countries lost $ 8.44 trillion to richer parts of the world through illegal transfers. The organisation estimated that $ 2.74 trillion or above 32 percent of the total loot was stolen from China. Given the generally strict control of the government, it is difficult to believe that they were totally unaware of the flow of this money from China. India is once again way behind China, with a loss of $ 125 billion.

Urban Bias, Abuse of Villages

We have already seen how people with an urban bias and no experience in and sympathy for the rural questions took over after the Tiananmen and allied urban uprisings of 1989. The agitations were expressions of urban discontent, which the leadership sought to appease quickly. The new leadership that assumed office after the military suppression of the countrywide troubles initiated fiscal centralisation to increase revenues, reduced provincial autonomy, tightened rural credit and closed down rural reforms. Over the next few years, the rural enterprises, the great symbols of free enterprise and the cradle of a truly home grown business class, began to fold up. Services in rural areas were charged, including for schooling and health care, thus reducing opportunities for economic advancement and social mobility. Household income, which grew at double digits, crawled at 0.7 percent for several years after 1989. Inevitably, peasants were driven to migrate, enlarging the labour market, depressing wages and primarily benefiting the overseas investors and the consumers in countries to which exports were made. The result was what Li Changping, the experienced rural cadre and critic of government policies whom we have met earlier, called the triple rural crisis of agriculture, governance, and peasantry caused by 'sharp income inequality, reduction in social opportunities in rural areas, slower income growth and an investment-heavy growth pattern'. Li Changping wrote a detailed letter to Premier Zhu Rongji with the bold and provocative title, '*I told the Premier the Truth*', which the Premier sent to his two deputies to examine. They read it and filed it away. Yes, the two deputies were Hu Jintao and Wen Jiabao, the President and Premier, respectively, of China from 2003 to 2013.

If rural income had grown later at the same pace as in the 1980s, they would have doubled in less than ten years. On the other hand, the poor became poorer as seen by the Gini Coefficient, which measures inequality. In 1978, it was 0.15, the sign of a highly egalitarian society. It had reached 0.43 in 2000 and 0.496 in 2006. China passed the USA and the UK several years back and became even more unequal than the traditionally very unequal Latin America. Li Changping summarized the situation thus, "In the 1980s, standard of living of peasants improved day by day and the level of tension was low in rural areas. In the 1990s, although rural economy continued to develop, the livelihood of peasants was difficult and the level of tensions in rural areas accelerated considerably."[33] Once again, we meet the watershed event of the Tiananmen uprising that brought a series of urban based politicians to power, who appeased the cities at the expense of the rural masses and created an even 'harder' state.

Even the change of government in 2012-13 has not shown any change in the composition of the leadership. Other than the President and the Premier, the five members of the Standing Committee of the Politburo, the final decision making authority, consist of the Party Secretaries of Shanghai, Tienjing, and Chongqing, all of them being cities with provincial status, plus the senior-most economic planner and the head of the Party Organisation Department in charge of files on all officials. There is none who deals with the vast countryside and the predominantly rural provinces of the interior in the highest decision making bodies.

The change in Party and government in 2002-03 made no significant changes in strategy. The two five year plans made frequent announcements about changing the focus of growth, but were bereft of fresh ideas. They rehashed phrases about rebalancing the economy, increasing the share of consumption, etc., but did nothing in practice. China continued to grow on the same old pattern, while Hu Jintao and Wen Jiabao continued to tread on water and let things coast along. That is why there is increasing concern that China could have a 'hard landing' because of a financial crisis and/or slower growth. As we have seen, China has inflicted a big damage on itself by drastic reduction in its labour force without upgrading its technical skills. The labour surplus will disappear by 2015. The slowing down of the markets in the West also leads to reduction in export led growth.

This is a combination that the new leadership that has assumed power will find hard to tackle. They may have to resort to a combination of measures like currency appreciation, increased taxation of government enterprises, boosting household income by refraining from compulsorily docking a part of their income in low interest bank accounts for investment, legalising migration to cities and even relaxing the one child policy. This would dampen exports and boost domestic consumption. However, the current arrangements are structural and hard to change because there are many entrenched bureaucracies with stakes in the status quo. One is not sure whether the new leadership can simultaneously take on the abortion bureaucracy, the banking system that thrives on pushing more and more credit, provincial governments that are addicted to FDI and use of low wage migrant workers.

We have already seen how the Party remains all pervading so that its control cannot be challenged. Given the extensive problems relating to environment, income disparities and intrusion into the personal space and rights of the people, the question arises as to how the Party keeps its grip and how it can continue to do so. It does so with a combination of comparative improvement in the welfare of the people that is reassuring to them and 'strike hard' – violent response to determined opposition.

Dissent in China

Discontent in China arises primarily from the land question, something familiar to us in India. Expropriation of land, especially agricultural land, for industrial use has led to massive agitations in our country. At the same time, these issues are also dealt with through a combination of judicial process and political agitations. They are both expensive when looked at purely in terms of opportunity cost of the projects, but have the virtue of producing solutions all can live with. As a minimum, they offer the satisfaction of getting the opportunity to argue one's case. This, of course, does not exist in China. The way Chinese judicial system operates is different. Cases are first considered by the Party and decided, in fact. Judiciary will pronounce only those sentences that are approved by the Party. The Chief Justice of China is a professional police officer with a degree in history, but no formal training in law. That tells us much about the judiciary (There are Party cells in courts for all 'judicial workers'). China uses death sentences extensively and carries them out without long drawn out scrutiny and appeals that are the hallmark of trials in most countries. More than 90 percent of executions worldwide are in China. It is said that transplantable organs are extracted from those executed and sold.

The 'reform through labour' camps, known in China as 'laogai', the Chinese version of the Russian gulag continues to exist despite the dismantling of most of what Mao built. That is where whistleblowers about corruption, dissidents, advocates of human rights, people who insist on suing the government, idealistic students etc. rub shoulders with murderers, rapists and embezzlers who escaped the death sentence. 'Counter-revolutionary activity', is a crime according to the criminal code adopted in 1979 when the Chinese government had abandoned the revolutionary principle. It is a catchall item because it is not defined exactly. So also with violation of 'state secrets', which includes (as a sample) "statistics of war dead and wounded since the Revolution, policy on land use, reports on environment, information on public health, reports on industrial accidents and ailments, unemployment and poverty data, accusations against national officials, statistics on strikes and demonstrations, data on national disasters and negative social phenomena that, once released, are not beneficial to human mind and society."[34] It is on the basis of this broad definition that doctors who exposed the AIDS that spread through the use of infected needles in hospitals and deaths from SARS virus, which became an epidemic in China, were punished. The official 'Legal Daily' acknowledged that 2.5 million people went through the system from 1957 to 1997 and that 280 laogai camps with 230,000 inmates existed in 1997. Harry Wu, a well known dissident estimated that more than 50 million would have gone through the camps. A recent account on the camps was written by Liao Yiwu, who was imprisoned for protesting the Tiananmen events. His narrative is quite similar to that of Harry Wu, who was in jail during the Mao era, showing that the camps form an integral part of the Chinese government system. The only difference is that guards and prison officials now keep the money coming from prisoners' labour in the spirit of Deng Xiaoping's dictum that it is glorious to be rich! Like the abolition of the residence permit system, the 13th Plenum also decided to do without the camps for reform through labour. Here again, the implementation of the formal decision will confront the government with hard challenges – how to reintegrate the hundreds of thousands, if not millions, who have been inmates of these camps for years. As in the case of the abortion bureaucracy, one can expect the bureaucracy of the camps too to delay the full realisation of the Party decision.

The advent of the internet complicates life for all autocracies. China has a very large number of netizens, though their number is exaggerated like all statistics from China. It is impressive, but is also an illustration of how stunted other media are for exchange of information and debate. Naturally, the government has a bureaucracy to monitor and sanitise the net. The net yet beats the authorities to the punch as in the case of the crash of the 'bullet train' in 2011 and the details connected to the disgrace of Politburo member Bo Xilai in 2012. It is a battle in which a ragtag collection of lawyers, journalists, entrepreneurs and artists struggle against the entrenched elite that tries to protect the authoritarian and venal Party state.

In the absence of any politically acceptable outlet for social frustrations and grievances, the only available means of expression is rioting. 'A riot is the language of the unheard' said Dr. Martin Luther King. (The historic right of the people to petition the Emperor is preserved in China where grievances can be brought to the attention of the centre by personally appearing in Beijing, but most of those who try that route would be arrested by local authorities when they try to board the train for the capital and clapped in jails.) Peasants have no choice when their land is taken away arbitrarily. Most of such confiscations also take place in the eastern part of the country, which is the only area, which can produce multiple crops in a year. This is the area of the EEZs, because it is close to Taiwan and Hong Kong, near ports, and was traditionally starved of investment in heavy industries. Demonstrations against authorities and resistance against arbitrary seizures of land came to be described as 'mass incidents', which have increased so much in number and intensity over the years that annual data ceased to be published after 2005. There were 58,000 incidents in 2003, 74,000 in 2004 and 87,000 in 2005. That is why there is a Public Security Bureau that is larger than the armed forces. No wonder the slogan of the past decade is social stability, status quo by another name. We are back to the imperial days of social harmony where everybody knew his place, and to paraphrase the Confucian dictum quoted in page 10, where the Politburo member is the Politburo member, the cadre is cadre, peasant is peasant, and migrant worker is migrant worker, the operation of a Confucian hierarchy by another name. No wonder there is no official data on 'mass incidents' though it is estimated that there are at least 100 large scale protest demonstrations every day in China in recent years.

Deng Xiaoping threw out the Maoist social model lock stock and barrel and retained only the coercive state apparatus. It is not that modernization and opening out were his discoveries. Opening to the USA, a precondition for the economic opening of the country, was a strategic turn by Mao. 'Four Modernisations were proposed by Zhou Enlai in 1975 when Mao was still alive. Deng made a target for 2000, the quadrupling of China's GNP. Mao too had a target for that year; in 1959, he said that by 2000, he hoped, China would have 'a strong socialist industrial economy capable of making a bigger contribution to mankind'. How interesting, how characteristic that Mao thought about a contribution to mankind, but his successor ignored 'mankind' and perhaps its Chinese portion too!

Chapter XI

Chauvinism and Targeting of Japan

Japan is the target of the worst of China's anger that hides much frustration. There are many reasons for China to hate Japan, thanks to the violence of its occupation of China and the misery that visited upon the Chinese between 1927 and 1945. Japan had defeated the Qing China in a war in Korea in 1895, exposing what a hollow giant China had become. Following that victory, Japan annexed Taiwan. After the First World War, Japan behaved no better than the Western nations in seeking concessions from China and using threats when negotiations failed. It was this incident involving Japan's demands that precipitated China's efforts to modernize, beginning with the celebrated May 4 Movement of 1919. This campaign was also a trigger for the establishment of the Communist Party in 1921.

The Communists had an axe to grind in claiming to be the sole force fighting the Japanese after they attacked China in 1931 and occupied a large part of the country by 1937 – a claim that reinforced their legitimacy. Like the many 'ifs' and the 'had it beens' of history, we need not speculate upon what would have happened if the Japanese had not taken on the USA, a move that resulted in the Americans smashing the Japanese war machine and leaving the Chinese continental space to be occupied by the Communists. The Soviet Union did not aid the Communist struggle, nor could we expect them to do it as they were engaged in a life and death struggle with the Nazis for sheer survival. At the same time, it is reasonable to assume that if Japan had not fought the USA, they would not have been dislodged from China that easily. As things are, the Second World War produced a good and useful enemy for the Communist Party. The hostility was maintained at a constant high pitch. For example, all the eight so called revolutionary operas sponsored by Mao's wife, Jiang Qing during the Cultural Revolution, had anti-Japanese struggle as background.

Japan rushed ahead of the USA to fully normalise relations with China in 1972. Prime Minister Kakuei Tanaka rushed to China in the wake of Henry Kissinger's secret visit. He met Mao and wished to express his apologies for Japan's misdeeds of the past. But Mao never gave him a chance to do so. He was able to ensure that he and China could hold Japan guilty of unexpiated war crimes and extract compensation through loans and grants of trillions of yen despite China waiving war reparations in their Peace Treaty (Among the Asian countries whose territories were occupied by Japan, only India waived war reparations before China did so). The loans and grants were acts of contrition and goodwill, but it never made any impression on China. Japanese aid projects are never identified as such. Chinese textbooks have not softened one bit on history. Browbeating continues about Japanese ministers visiting the shrine where their military men who died fighting for the country are honoured. Japanese have reacted with hesitation till recently when the current Prime Minister Shinzo Abe has finally chosen to take a line of not being too apologetic. Soccer games with Japan, which the latter usually wins, are special moments for fierce displays of hatred. There is even an entire Museum on atrocities perpetrated by Japan. Is there a reason for fanning such fierce flames of hatred when so much of time has passed?

There is; and the point is psychological. Historically, Japan borrowed so much from China – its script which they still call the kanji or Han letters, poetic styles, painting tradition, the Confucian ethos. Buddhism reached Japan from China including Zen, which was called Chan (which, in turn, is the Chinese version of Dhyan). Even the traditions that are considered indelible parts of Japanese culture like the tea ceremony, the board game called Weiqi, which is called 'Go' in Japan, and even the flower arrangement of Ikebana, are all Chinese in origin. How many of these are alive in China today and how many are there where the Chinese are the best practitioners? Sadly, hardly any! Not even calligraphy, the most elegant of traditional Chinese arts where the Chinese chose to display on the monument to the revolutionary martyrs at the Tiananmen Square in Beijing and on the masthead of the *People's Daily* the inelegant scrawl of Mao Zedong, a poor model to imitate. The Japanese Emperor's court holds annual poetry and calligraphy contests, but nothing similar is heard from China. Zen went to China from India and had its headquarters in Shaolin Mountains, but it is not even heard of now in that country, while it flourishes in Japan. Japan is ultra modern; yet it is so traditional that its National Zoo in Tokyo holds a meet once a year to pray for peace of the souls of the animals that died in the zoo the previous year.

The point is that Japan is a humiliating reminder of all that China could have become, but didn't. Japan is a relatively small country that borrowed so much from China, but made it all its own. At the same time, Japan did not lose its identity at any point of time. Later, it synthesised its identity with modernity to become a prosperous and harmonious country, which even survived a horrible war without an internal revolution. Democratic consensus works in Japan. The society was never corrupt and the civil service is clean and dedicated, working on the basis of the Confucian principle of virtuous example. Social inequalities are negligible and a conscious effort is made to ensure that it stays so. Knowledge and innovation are encouraged and respected. Japan has learned its lessons from the misdeeds of the past and has accepted its medicine. In Japan, changes took place without the violence, revolution and civil war that took place in China. In the 19th century, some groups did fight to resist the changes being brought about by the Meiji Restoration, but there was never the kind of violence involving masses of people as in the repeated Chinese political campaigns. Political assassinations were frequent in the 1930s, but Japan never had anything like the Cultural Revolution in which even top level leaders were done to death. Therefore, the reaction of present day China to Japan displays all the signs of inferiority complex, a sense that all that was theirs has been mindlessly thrown away to create a life that is poorer culturally and at disproportionate cost. Liao Yiwu, the poet, who was thrown into the gulag, whom we had met already, spent his prison days gluing labels to medicine packets when he was not being tortured. He imagined "the entire country gluing medicine packets all day. This is our brave new world," a situation in which the political prison mimicked China and vice versa. A person with a chip on the shoulder becomes a bully, in fact, all bullies have chips on the shoulder.

We in India do not have the burden of either having borrowed anything from China or having harmed it in any manner. However, can we not also say that in some respects, we too are what China did not become? We too should make up our minds on this question once we have completed the various elements of this review. That could perhaps throw more light on how we look at each other because that could clear our mind about what we are so that we can see China from our own perspective.

An Explanation for the Insecurity

In the earlier part of this essay, we had seen that China had taken pride in its culture which had developed without borrowing anything significant from anywhere, without coming into conflict with and being challenged by another civilisation culturally or intellectually and remaining confident of its superiority in all spheres, being surrounded by either nomadic tribes not worthy of their concern or smaller states treated as unimportant entities. We have also seen how this self image received a mortal wound in the 19th century beginning with the two 'Opium Wars' of 1840 and 1860, which imposed treaties on China after battles, which exposed not only China's military fragility against industrialised countries, but also laid bare the distrust between the Qing rulers and their Chinese subjects, as quite a few Chinese either remained indifferent to or actively helped the British in their campaigns against the Qing Empire. This was followed by the Boxer Rebellion of 1900 when the troops from Britain, France, Russia, The USA, Germany, Japan, Italy and Austria (take Austria away and add Canada and you get the G 8, as Deng Xiaoping saw it!). This was a deeply humiliating experience for the Chinese intellectuals and political leaders of all persuasions. That is why a concept of 'national humiliation' arose in China, initially propagated by the militant youth following the May 4 Movement of 1919 – the beginning of the national effort to modernise China – and carefully promoted as an idea for mass mobilisation and to justify a strong and authoritarian government, first by the Guomindang and then by the Communist Party, as a requirement to avenge this condition. However, China remained divided among local warlords and was also partly occupied by Japan in the first half of the 20th century. The country achieved unity once again only when the People's Republic was founded in 1949. Thus, they could consider the hundred years prior to the proclamation of the People's Republic to be 'a century of humiliation'.

Marking this period with a day of recollection started in the days of the Guomindang. This has continued in some manner even after the Communist victory. At present, the third Saturday of September is dedicated to recalling the past humiliations through National Defence Education days. Each achievement of China in science, economy, or industrial production is emphatically celebrated, especially if it involves comparison with the USA, because the government is able to tell the people that these are the examples of erasing of the century of humiliation. This is, of course, something unusual, even unique, among nations. This campaign also helps the regime by diverting attention from disasters inflicted on China by its own governments during the Civil War, the Great Leap Forward, the Great Famine, the Cultural Revolution and the suppression of the democracy movement of

1989 by using the military. For example, the government quickly changed the discourse after 1989 by unleashing a propaganda barrage to remember the 150th anniversary of the Opium War. This was the start of a major ideological campaign lasting many years, aiming 'to boost the nation's spirit, enhance its cohesion, foster its self esteem and sense of pride, consolidate and develop a patriotic united front' as the *People's Daily* formulated it. Analysing these trends, Julia Lovell concludes that the 'campaign encompassed three big ideas: first, to indoctrinate the Chinese in the idea that China possessed a unique, glorious, millennia-old 'national condition' (*guoqing*) unready for democracy; second, to remind them of their sufferings at the hand of the West; and third, to underline the genius of the Communist leadership'.[36] At the same time, despite the use of films and other mass media, the results have been ambivalent at best because of the decreasing trust of the masses in the party, an awareness that China was humiliated because of its own fecklessness, and, most important of all, the deep interest in the West and all that it stands for politically and intellectually among the youth, who were the main targets of such propaganda.

Yan Xuetong published a book entitled *Unhappy China* in 2009. This widely read book is an excellent illustration of some common trends in Chinese attitudes that are neither well known nor much reported in our country. He observed that 'the sole, dominant ideology shared by the government and the people is money worship .... Our military budget is already 1.6 times that of the Russians, but we cannot build the same military. Our education spending is much larger than India's, but we cannot have one single person win the Nobel Prize. They already have ten. We have more rich people than Japan and we have more first ranked companies, but we can't build world class products. We have more foreign exchange reserves than anyone else, but we cannot build a financial centre even like Hong Kong.' While one can quibble about the correctness of the number of Nobel Prize winners from India, and hope that Mo Yan's prize would reduce his anguish, the point made by Yan Xuetong throws a lot of light on the obsessions of the Chinese, something much at variance with the image we have of that country.

Chinese leaders talk much about 'China's rightful place' in the world, an expression of a sense of entitlement that is encouraged by all the talk in Western media about it being the next superpower. They also expect others to endorse this frequently. Part of this is the mentality of 'middle kingdom' that expects tributes, part of it is a mask for its insecurities. Another posture is to snarl at enemies, as we have seen in relation to Japan. So also with the Dalai Lama and those, who receive him, etc. It is only in China that holding the Olympics is seen as proving 'not only the existence of a China model, but of its success'[35] and the Games proving to be a 'heavy blow to the self confidence of Western values' and the settling of 100 years of national humiliation.

The second part of this program is to harp on how colonialism took away territories from China – areas that the Chinese say was 'always part of China', which range from the whole of South East Asia, Mongolia, Russian Maritime Province, Nepal, Bhutan, parts of India claimed by China, parts of Central Asian Republics, the islands in the South China Sea, the Ryukyus of Japan, and, occasionally Afghanistan too. Nothing is, of course, said about Chinese annexation of various territories because they too were 'always part of China'. Sometimes, this boomerangs as South Korean scholars deem Korean speaking areas in northeast China to be Korean lands.

Chapter XII

China and the USA

As we have seen already, Mao assessed the situation of China and took the strategic decision to open up to the USA. It was a big decision, but, for the USA too, it was a big decision. That decision was to bring China into the world system that was shaped by the USA after World War II of which the pillars were the UN, World Bank, IMF and GATT (later the WTO). We also recall that the USA achieved an agreement on the establishment of relations with China without compromising on any of its premises on regional security, like alliance with Japan, protection of South Korea and Taiwan from armed attacks, and military guarantees to its friends in South East Asia. These old positions have been strengthened now with good relations with Vietnam, a call to China to resolve its boundary disputes in South China Sea without resorting to arms, and an insistence that the freedom of navigation in that area be maintained undisturbed. China has accepted all these premises and stipulations. In retrospect, normalisation of relations with China on its own terms was a significant victory for America vis-a-vis a country that was fiercely hostile only a few years earlier.

There is much written about China confronting the US as its economy grows. There is nothing to show that a large economy should flex its muscles because it is a large economy. The Soviet Union confronted the US because it represented an alternative to the USA in political philosophy and organisation of economy. That is not true of China, which is integrated with the global financial and supply chain arrangements. Nor does China offer itself as an alternative to American capitalism and as an alternative model for other countries. Some parallels have been drawn between China-US relations and UK-Germany relations of early 20th century. The lesson is even more obvious in this case. When Germany challenged Britain, she was confronted by a huge coalition that beat it. It is virtually impossible for a challenger to organize a coalition to fight the current hegemon because the hegemonic country can break the coalition by splitting it bit by bit and by isolating and destroying the challenger. Therefore, there is nothing inevitable about a conflict between China and the US. At least in public, China is committed to 'peaceful rise'.

There are people and groups in both the countries who spoil for a fight. Max Boot has argued that there is both 'good' and 'bad' China bashing; checking China's competitiveness is bad, but checking its military build-up is good (of course from the American point of view). Kissinger has argued that a Cold War with the US will have a 'potentially catastrophic impact … on the continued rising of the standard of living on which the legitimacy of the government depends'. The US would like China to be helpful in pressurising North Korea on its nuclear program, stopping the theft of intellectual property and terminating hacking to steal trade secrets. There are similar demands from China too including the demand to stop snooping on its military by the US.

Nixon, the old master of strategy and realpolitik understood all this and laid it out concisely prior to his negotiations with Mao. He made three lists. 'What they wanted' were: 1) build up their credentials in the world, 2) Taiwan, and 3) get US out of Asia. 'What we wanted' were: 1) Indo-china?, 2) communications – restrain Chinese expansion in Asia, 3) reduce future threat of confrontation by superpower China. The third list of what both wanted was 1) reduce confrontation and conflict, 2) more stable Asia, and 3) restrain USSR.[37] It is striking that a wealthy China was taken as a given by Nixon when he described it as a superpower as far back as 1972 and it did not appear to him as a menace. It is obvious that he saw the gains from trade and China's integration into the world, whose rules were framed and implemented by the USA, far outweighing any military threat from it. The list shows how consistent successive US administrations have been in dealing with China and how successful they have been in achieving their objectives. By helping the formation of ASEAN and supporting those countries protect themselves against Chinese subversion, the US got its third aim. Even on 'Indo-china' where Nixon could not go beyond a question mark, the US has been successful in the long run as Vietnam has developed good relations including military cooperation with the US.[38]

China has been non-confrontational with the US. In the 1970s, they operated under a tacit defense umbrella of the US while facing the Soviet Union. They helped the US in the Cold War by tying up a million Soviet soldiers and received satellite intelligence as quid pro quo. They lowered the decibel levels on Taiwan and have now reconciled themselves to a de facto independent existence of that island. The low wage migrants helped the US keep a consumer boom. China kept most of its foreign exchange in US Treasury securities and helped fund the US budget deficit. As the Chinese currency appreciates, the money earned by the toils of the Chinese workers reduces in value. Though there are many ways in which the Chinese could have used the funds, they have chosen to invest in US government. It is a voluntary act and as the decision of the Central Bank, very much a political decision to help the US. China also has a strong interest in the continued welfare of the US because a collapse of the US would mean that China will have to write off most of its foreign exchange hoard.

It should, in fairness, be added that China has taken very carefully prepared steps for wider use of yuan so that it is not necessary to rely solely on the US Treasury. These measures include: a) designating trade in yuan, b) schemes for portfolio investments, c) development of offshore yuan markets in Hong Kong, Singapore, and London and d) currency swap arrangements with Hong Kong,

Brazil, South Korea, European Union, UK, Australia, Brazil, etc. It is estimated that 17 percent of China's trade was settled in yuan in 2013. It is still a small amount compared to the volume of transactions in US dollars. China still has capital controls; its currency trades within a narrow band determined officially rather than being traded freely, and there are severe regulations on banking. China is also handicapped by huge debts incurred by local governments and municipalities estimated at more than $ 3 trillion and other significant debts by firms. At the same time, the gradual and calibrated efforts by China will continue and, in the light of China's position as the largest trading nation and a major investor internationally (China's external investment has been more than Us $ 60 billion in 2012 and 2013), yuan's importance as a reserve currency is bound to increase gradually.

Role of the PLA

The role of the PLA is also worth reviewing in the context of China-US relations. Military modernisation was one of the four modernizations of Deng Xiaoping. It was also needed because of the pathetic performance of the PLA when it launched an attack on Vietnam in 1979 'to teach a lesson'. However, one is not sure how well it will do in battle even after massive investment over the last three decades. In all these years it has not shot in anger at an enemy since it botched the attack on Vietnam and was badly mauled. After all, the only engagement of the PLA since Vietnam has been at the Tiananmen in 1989 against its own unarmed people. The PLA, which reached its maximum size of 4.75 million in 1981, was made leaner by Deng Xiaoping, who fixed a retirement age and sent surplus officers to run businesses. We have also seen how military is involved in many activities unrelated to war fighting.

The reform and professionalisation of the PLA continued under Jiang Zemin and Hu Jintao. Unlike Deng, who had the rank of a General from 1947 as the political commissar in the army of Liu Bocheng, the most renowned strategist of the PLA, the two later leaders ran purely civilian regimes. They humoured the PLA with double digit increases in military budget and let the armed forces buy as much weapons as it wanted, but also abandoned an armed race and gave up the policy of capturing Taiwan by force. Party control over the army increased; the PLA could no longer create foreign policy situations as in the 1960s and embarrass the Party and the government.

The civilian leadership is aware that the Party could lose control over a professional PLA. That is why the 2.3 million strong armed forces have no less than 90,000 Party cells. PLA presence in the Politburo has been whittled down. No serving soldier has been a member of the Standing Committee of the Politburo since 1992. PLA gets a lot of money to buy stuff, but is on a tight leash on the policy front so that nothing is done to jeopardise the peaceful environment in which China has prospered in the last four decades.

In practice, China is bottled up behind mountains, deserts, and a chain of islands that stretch almost unbroken from Sakhalin in the north through Japan, Taiwan, the Philippines, all the way to Indonesia. All these countries and the USA are aware that control of any of these islands by the Chinese would open the Pacific for the Chinese navy. They will do all that is possible to prevent such an eventuality. China has commissioned its first carrier, but that alone is not going to make a big difference. Hence, the drumbeat about the islands in South China Sea and the mythology about Zheng He's voyages dominating the Indian Ocean! At the same time, China made a quick promise to talk about the islands as soon as the US Secretary of State rejected sovereignty claims, lowered tensions and even allowed Chinese scholars to write scoffing at China's claims to the islands. The Chinese pushed their claims; when the Americans pushed back, they retreated, offered to talk and eased their rhetoric. We can see a pattern that is not going to change very soon.

Thus, there is little evidence to show that China is engaged in a path of confrontation with the US or would do anything to destabilize the relationships the USA has built up in East and Southeast Asia. The US also maintains strong economic relationships through multilateral arrangements, like APEC and is working on free trade agreements with most of countries in the region. China is also heavily dependent on the US markets, another incentive for it not to do anything destabilising. Even in the UN, China has so far not done anything that has directly obstructed what the US has considered to be its vital interest.

Chapter XIII

China's Traditions, Open Markets, and One Party Rule – How They Add Up

China's Idea of China

We have seen in the earlier part of this essay the various elements that have gone into what China is, its almost entirely home-made culture, its tendency to create a strong and centrally ruled state, which is run by a bureaucracy that is dedicated to an official ideology, its belief that law emerges from the ruler rather than being a separate and abstract entity, its imperviousness to external influences and the resultant autonomy of thought and action that is ingrained because of historic limitations of continuous contacts with other cultures. How much of these have survived and how are these habits of thought and behaviour relevant today?

The People's Republic has appropriated the imperial idea of China ("a civilisation pretending to be a nation" in the words of Lucien Pye) by reinventing the 2500 year old autocracy to control the populace and hector other countries. China developed nuclear weapons which is a big power attribute these days. The Qing Empire has been recreated now and it has been drilled into the minds of its own people that China "always" looked like the Qing Empire, thus justifying the annexation of Xinjiang and Tibet at certain points of time. That is why the government did not allow the depiction of the map of China during the Ming era in the Chinese translation of the *Cambridge History of China*. China also uses its sheer bulk to intimidate when it chooses. The hectoring and indignant tone that is adopted when it chooses is also part of its armoury. The oldest and biggest country, which also has the biggest grievance for being badly treated in the past, has a natural right to be indignant. Though others are no longer called 'mosquitoes and scorpions' as the first Ming Emperor dubbed the Japanese and Vietnamese, the Chinese could still call a Japanese Prime Minister 'a notorious prostitute, who insists on a monument erected to her own chastity', and call us 'reactionary clique' and 'expansionists'. Zhou Enlai lectured Nehru (The Chinese created an impression that Nehru patronised Zhou in Bandung, but let us listen to what Zhou had to say later, "Nehru was an arrogant man. He took me around and introduced me as though Zhou Enlai needed introduction" - not the Chinese Premier, but Zhou Enlai! Now, who was arrogant?).

Equally symptomatic is the way the government is intolerant of any ceding of space to any authority even on matters that are not in the province of a modern civilian government. The Chinese government makes the incomprehensible assertion that it will decide who the next Dalai Lama will be in the company of the Communist Party. The government appoints bishops of the Chinese Catholic Church and refuses to recognise those appointed by the Pope. The Chairman's authority over his people is as absolute as that of the Yellow Emperor. It shows externally when it boasts about its military strength, talks about 'teaching a lesson' to others, and its obsessive comparisons with the USA. On the other hand, the West also had its own perceptions and objectives.

Let us now tie up the argument we started with, that Western scholarship and media had a specific agenda, when they pushed the line that opening of China to capitalist development through massive investment from abroad has been a great and unmitigated blessing for China. Such an opening was the fond wish of both the Missionary and the Merchant for a long time. The Missionary came in two varieties, the spiritual, who wanted to save the souls of the Chinese and his modern variation, who wanted to turn the face of the Chinese towards the true path to prosperity through capitalist development. The Merchant was an ally of both type of missionaries, but had the narrow agenda of getting rich. When the People's Republic faced an impasse in its developmental experiment following its break with the Soviet Union and its foreign policy of promoting armed revolution was checked, there was a great policy turnaround resulting in a realignment that coincided with the objectives of both the secular Missionary and the Merchant. It committed China to a not easily revocable long term strategy of offering its large labour force at very inexpensive rates to foreign investors for the production of goods for export at attractive rates for consumption in developed countries. The re-creation of Shanghai as a government-developed city, as the base for foreign capital was a key element in this strategy, an action that brought to full circle the process of the forced opening of China initiated a century and half back, reversed by the socialist policies implemented by Mao after the Liberation, and reversed again by his successors.

The flow of cheap labour to the cities was engineered by making life in rural areas increasingly unattractive through additional expenses and levies. China also made foreign investment attractive through preferential laws for investors and EEZs. This strategy was successful in releasing the surplus labour in the countryside by opening up fresh opportunities for the surplus labour and bettering living conditions, thus obtaining the consent of the governed – the modern mandate from Heaven – for the Party to continue its arbitrary grip on power. This situation suits the countries that invest in China because, by now, China's commitment to the strategy was irrevocable and its entanglement with the capitalist free trading system inextricable. It is natural for the media in these countries to extol China as a great model.

We have found what price China has paid for this strategy in environmental degradation. It should be remembered that despite all the western talk about China's hardware and India's software; China's hardware, for that matter, most of its industrial production, is assembly. Yan Xuetong's lament about China not producing any brand product is a valid one. Apple carefully writes that it is designed in California and assembled in China. This is a major limitation of China. The third problem is that the surplus labour that was pushed out of the villages to run the manufacturing machine and amass the foreign exchange hoard is not infinite. One child policy has ensured that this will taper off quite soon. What happens after that? Can China get foreign investment at the current rate of more than $100 billion year after year?

China cannot compare itself with Japan or South Korea, not to mention Taiwan or Singapore, because China is corrupt unlike all of them. Authoritarianism in Korea and Japan was benevolent for their people. Even a military dictator like Park Chung Hee of Korea was a personally clean man. Legal procedures are fair and transparent. The same qualities obtain in Singapore, a one Party State for all practical purposes, where decision making is honest and law and business practices are transparent. Progress was achieved in all of them without violence towards people, without dishonouring their traditions. That stands in stark contrast as a moral and ethical challenge to the means adopted by the Chinese Party to try to arrive at similar ends. We have also seen how Confucian traditions reached Korea and Japan and remain alive as normal habits and mode of conduct. The result is that Korea and China enriched their culture through borrowing from China, but never lost their quintessential native spirits, but for China to become a spiritual desert that knows only the GNP and 'peaceful rise' but little else. That is why Qian Xuesen, the celebrated 'father of the Chinese bomb', lamented to Premier Wen Jiabao, 'We need more innovation. We are not producing any creative people. We are making only technicians'. Liu Xiaobo, the dissident, who was imprisoned later and was conferred the Nobel Prize for Peace while in prison, made a similar assessment, "The society is becoming even more superficial … we grew up in a desert."[39] China also became a far more unequal society than all its neighbours, both richer and poorer of them.

We also discovered how China is a republic without being a democracy and how democratic experiments there withered again and again. Can the present arrangements continue forever? Will there be an upheaval? One cannot make predictions because, in such societies, the tipping point is reached well before it is recognised. Such governments cannot easily reform themselves. The accuracy of Alexis de Tocqeville's well known observation that "the most perilous moment for a bad government is when it seeks to reform its ways," is proved by the experiences of the Bourbons, who were overthrown by the French revolution, the Czar, the Shah of Iran and the Soviet Union. The Chinese would be aware of all these precedents, which perhaps explains their policy of 'strike hard', the way Tiananmen and all similar activities are handled, the harsh punishments inflicted on activists in defiance of world public opinion, and restrictions on internet and other forms of free communication. Writing about the prospects of democracy in China, Bruce Gilley observes that 'nobody has brought a Leninist state through the Scylla of reforming and losing control and the Charybdis of not reforming and losing support." At the same time, China is not a standard issue Communist State, but the oldest of states with extremely well tested instruments of power and well honed reflexes to administrative challenges. The post-communist state is structured no differently from the empire of the past with an ideologically motivated bureaucracy loyal to the all powerful Party, which is led by a leader in whose hands all power is concentrated. The state is, in fact, stronger now than at any time in the past because it can use all new technologies like roads, railways, telecommunications, and internet for more effective control. New instruments of mass persuasion like nationalism, unknown in the past, are also available in the government's arsenal for deployment. The government also allows those who want to merely get along to do so, vacating some space for people's privacy, unlike in the Communist days, when everybody was compelled to get involved in every campaign. This will allow the state to roll along the same path with little demand for change. That is why Min Xinpei, the most serious student of the subject, came to the conclusion that the country will neither implode nor change, but muddle through.[40]

What are the dangers of muddling through? Slowing down of the economy would be the most obvious danger. All indications point to a slowdown and it appears that the government is reconciled to it and is trying to get the people used to it the way President Xi is now talking about GNP not being everything. It has been assumed for long that nine percent growth is essential for the stability of the regime. The first casualties of the slowdown would be the youth looking for work. Already graduates in China wait for more than a year on an average before they can hope for work. How will further slowdown affect them, and what kind of sops can the government offer to keep them calm? It is a serious challenge to the new leadership that assumed office only in 2012-13.

What would be the belief system that would motivate Xi Jinping, Li Keqiang and others of their generation? Born in the first decade after Liberation, they all grew up, princelings and paupers' sons, believing in the Revolution and in the motto 'Serve the People', the title of a speech by Mao that everybody in China used to memorise and recite from memory in the '60s. As boys and girls, they saw or even took part in the suppression of the landlord class. The paupers' sons would also have seen the extensive starvation deaths in the countryside between 1959 and 1961, and those, who survived the famine and reached a high position in the Party would know that they are party to a lie when the Party claims even today that bad weather or the falling out with the Soviet Union caused some deaths in those years. By the time they became teenagers, in 1966, Mao told them that most of the leaders they revered, including his own father in the case of Xi Jinping (and so many other children of cadres) were actually 'traitors and scabs', who are to be struggled against. They became Red Guards with much enthusiasm to fight, abuse and torture those whom they admired and respected till the previous day. Today's China is full of stories of remorse of the young of those days who denounced their parents in this atmosphere of frenzy, condemning them to death or a not much better fate of long periods of imprisonment and reform through labour. When they were no longer of such use and were floating around in cities without work, Mao gathered them and sent them off to the countryside to 'stay for a long time and learn from poor and lower middle peasants'. The majority became the 'lost generation' without a chance for good education and opportunity for a decent life. Some able and lucky individuals reached college, when institutes of higher education reopened after a gap of several years in 1975. By the time they were around 30, the new leadership, which got rid of those who came to power during the Cultural Revolution, told them that the 1966 campaign was all wrong and was contrary to the Party's principles even when the new leaders remained unwilling to point the finger at Mao as the source of the turmoil. They were told that 'getting rich was glorious', negating all that they learned as boys and girls. How has this generation reacted to truth as proclaimed by the Party being reversed after ten years and the reversal being reversed after another ten years? Would it have been normal for them to become cynical and get rich as best as they can, get ahead in life anyway they can, principles be damned? Most of them had seen grinding poverty as children and, after the twists and turns of their young days, could anybody blame them if they thought that making money matters and not much else, especially because they were also the generation on whom the one child policy was inflicted first on top of everything else? This is the age cohort from which the current Politburo is chosen. What is the implication of the leadership of a very large country, a leadership, which is ensured a long tenure and does not have to test its policies constantly against the touchstone of public opinion, emerging from such a cohort whose experience tells them not to accept and trust any ideology and who rose in rank in an atmosphere of self preservation and self aggrandisement?

Chapter XIV

India and China: Conclusions from this Survey

Weiqi: The Game the Chinese Play

Before we return to our initial concern of trying to find an Indian point of view on China, we also have to be introduced to weiqi (वेय छी), a well known board game that originated in China and is still played there. A board game enters the area of strategy precisely because it is a great game of strategy whose principles inspire the habits of Chinese strategic thinking. Weiqi can be translated as 'encirclement chess'. It is called 'Go' by the Japanese who have refined the theory of the game and have become masters of it as with many things Chinese. The Chinese also have the standard chess game with two interesting additions - a river in the middle of the board separating the two sides, a Rubicon that many pieces cannot recross, and two pieces of artillery per side that naturally capture by jumping over an intervening piece. But weiqi is an entirely different game, ancient in origin, played especially by military men and taken so seriously as a strategic game that Marshal Chen Yi, military hero of the Civil War and long time Foreign Minister was the President of the Weiqi Federation.

Its importance for military strategy is shown in the book, *Protracted Game: Weiqi Interpretation of Maoist Revolutionary Strategy*, written by Scott A Boorman, a Harvard mathematician and expert on China's internal political affairs, in which he compares the weiqi game with the guerrilla tactics adopted by the PLA in the anti-Japanese war in the 1940s. Thus, he demonstrated that weiqi thinking influences military tactics. Weiqi is what is called a 'perfect information game' by game theorists. It is played by mathematicians and military generals in the USA, for instance. Those readers familiar with Sylvia Nasr's biography of John Nash, the mathematician who won the Economics Nobel, would recall several references to the game in that book. It is unfortunate that our strategists who study and speak frequently on China, appear to be utterly unaware of this game. The nearest our generals have got to 'Go' is golf.

Weiqi is played on aboard marked with 19 squares horizontally and vertically, making for 361 points of intersections. There are black and white pieces but, unlike in chess, all pieces called stones are identical. They are placed on the intersections, not in the squares as chess pieces are. Black makes the first move. Once placed in a square, they do not move. The purpose of the game is to link the pieces in such a manner that stones belonging to a side are connected to form a territory that cannot be breached, encircled, or individual stones captured. Links are formed by stones in adjoining intersections in straight lines. As stones do not move, they can be played anywhere on the board. Just as one makes an interlinked territory, one also tries to immobilise the enemy stones, prevent their linkage, and, if needed, surround and capture them. As the game is played over the entire board, several battles and skirmishes take place simultaneously, defending, expanding one's territory or encircling enemy stones, with the possibility that different battles could join up and large groups of stones could be lost if the game is played without strategic planning. When the majority of stones are played and no more can be played to one's advantage, the game comes to an end. Then, the intersections controlled by each side are counted and the winner is decided on the obvious basis of which side controls the larger number of intersections.

It must be remembered that the loser does not surrender as in chess, whose king is checkmated or is about to be checkmated, thus losing everything. Here the loss is relative. The loser has his territory that is unconquered and is safely his. It is a protracted game of position, entrenched strongholds that push out from the edges to surround and strangle the foe, and determined domination of space through the creation of linkages among apparently isolated groups in different parts of the board.

Boorman demonstrates that weiqi thinking is natural to the Chinese strategists. He describes the progress of a battle in the Chinese Civil War and compares it with an actual weiqi game. The above description will have also made it amply clear that it is a war game and the study of weiqi would offer us not only insights into Chinese thinking, but suggest ideas for points of action. The game is, thus, fit to be played in the international board just as much as over the game board. In the international board too, one can set up unbreachable strong points, use a small group to tie up larger enemy forces engaged and achieve one's aims through the most economical use of power, avoid close combats, assess situations on the basis of cold calculations so that one can give up lost positions early without wasting more resources in such dubious battles, and gradually dominate the board. The readers would now have a very good idea of the possibilities and the options that are available to us.

What should We Do?

It should be clear by now that India and China are put together and governed in very different styles, thus creating very different kinds of governments, political systems, approaches to the construction of social harmony, attitudes to rights of people, interactions with the rest of the world and contents of their self definition as nations and states.

It is also true, as the earlier part of this has shown, that Indians and Chinese have been strangers to each other for most of history and have hardly had any experience of cultural and intellectual exchange, except for the journey of Buddhism to China where it was never an integral part of the mainstream unlike in Japan and Korea. This is in sharp contrast with our contacts with all the other civilisations of the past – Egyptian, Mesopotamian, Greek, Iranian, etc. We knew all of them to some measure. In the modern times, leaving aside the immense intellectual influence of the West with which we share our ideals of liberty, equality and justice, the concepts of democracy and impartiality of law that are derived from those ideals, our give and take with other cultures are significant. People of Indian origin living in the US buttress our good relations. Iranians are our neighbours with whom we share language, cuisine, and architecture. In addition to the commonalities of faith that a large segment of our people share with Iran and the Arab nations, we have considerable cultural and human contacts with the entire world of Islam. The great literature of Russia inspired our writers and the principles of the October Revolution are guiding many in our country. Japan is admired for the delicacy of arts, the high quality of its technology and its friendship in sharing it with us for the benefit of our people. None of this applies to China. Among all the big countries and cultural regions of the world, for the people of India, China is the one country that is the least known, the one country that has left the least mark on our ethos, the mental makeup of our people. Therefore, it would be very difficult for any government in India to develop relations with China on the basis of an established reservoir of goodwill towards China among the people of our country, the sense of identification and solidarity that would help overcome conflicts.

As demonstrated already, we became neighbours only after 1950 when Tibet became a part of China and came to be strongly controlled by China. It was this 'hard' control, quite characteristic of Chinese style of governance, that created the initial conditions for the confrontation of the two countries in the absence of a precisely drawn border. Our experience as neighbours has not been a happy one, a situation that is harder to resolve because of the mental distance of the two countries from each other. China also had the problem of never having lived cheek by jowl with another nation of long and well entrenched culture, thanks to which they spoke to us in the language of the empire to the vassal, a language obviously unacceptable to us. We have also seen how China hectors others, which is not a sign of strength, but of insecurity. This is manifested in our case by the endless demands that we say, on each and every occasion, that Tibet is a part of China. Why should we do so, again and again, when the Chinese assert huffily on other occasions and to other countries that Tibet is an internal matter in which no one else has any business to interfere?

We have also noted the potential pitfalls in the continuation of the current development strategy that awaits China. The economic slowdown in the rest of the world, as well as the thinning of its own workforce would reduce China's growth. The Party relies on growth for its continued right to rule. A slowdown could increase disaffection, particularly of the educated unemployed, which could become violent in the absence of democratic channels of expression. This is not a prediction, but a statement of possibility. If it comes to pass, it is not to be gloated over. Our humane tradition demands that we should not wish suffering on the people of China who have suffered things unimaginable to us in the last hundred years and have at last reached the threshold of a decent life. Nor is it in our interest because it is an empirically tested fact that Chinese authorities lash out abroad when they are in domestic trouble. When we are engaged in the primary task of improving the condition of our own people, increased problems with China should be avoided. Therefore, let us hope that the Chinese economy does not suffer what is called a 'hard landing' and create a situation in which the government tries to distract the people with the search of an external enemy.

Not that China is short of such potential enemies. They have confronted all their neighbours in Southeast Asia by claiming the entire South China Sea to be their sovereign territory, thus taking their borders to the very coasts of Vietnam, the Philippines and

Malaysia. They have escalated the war of words and occasionally arms, with Japan, their favourite foe. However, the present Japanese government has not reacted with hesitation, but with determination. All these developments have led the USA, the guardian of the Pacific, to come to the diplomatic aid of the Southeast Asian nations. China has much to worry with these simmering tensions.

If we apply the principles of weiqi that we studied in the earlier part of this chapter, we could conclude that the time is ripe to deal with the border. Before we come to the positive reasons for doing so, let us respond to some popular alternatives and show that they are not feasible or viable.

One popular argument is that we should establish solidarity with China in the spirit of the Asian century, developing country solidarity, etc. We have shown that China never cared for such alliances and had always behaved as an autonomous power. It is also conscious of being a 'big power'. It no longer says that it is part of the 'third world'. Therefore, this route, an attempted re-creation of the 'Bandung spirit' in a 21st century version, will lead us nowhere.

Another popular line is that we strengthen our military linkages with the US, expand contacts with Japan, Australia etc. and increase pressure on China. When there was a brief faceoff between the troops of the two countries in April-May 2013, some 'strategist' even predicted that the event would lead to closer links with the US. He was of course articulating his own wish in the guise of strategy because the government wisely and patiently resolved the matter without violence and without concessions. It should also be obvious to the readers of this essay that this is part of the Western agenda. Recall that the change of development strategy in China from socialist to foreign investment driven was hailed by the Western press as a model for all. China was also the much admired big prize. Therefore, it suits them to say that China will get stronger and stronger compared to us, leaving us with permanent disadvantages, in a situation in which we have no option but to lean on the West. This is quite an insidious argument because there is a powerful group of people in this country that is ready to vend this line.

This line sells because it suits many constituencies, those who still believe that they can settle the score for 1962, those committed to military tie ups with the US, Israel etc., the lobbies, who wish to sell even more arms and, most importantly, our own armed forces, who will become a larger player in the formulation of policy in such a scenario. The decision to raise more mountain troops, made in the wake of the brief confrontation in April-May 2013, is an example of how such incidents can lead to large and expensive decisions. While most of the media commentary urged an escalation in the faceoff, the Chinese reacted calmly to the news of the raising of additional divisions. The game of escalation can be played by both. The Chinese remained calm perhaps because they felt that they could match and more than match any escalation by us. How long and how far can it go? Where will it end?

Though we fought a brief war more than fifty years back, the India-China border, which is not demarcated, is far quieter than the well demarcated borders with Pakistan and even Bangladesh. We can thank the agreements on the maintenance of peace on the border for that. If skirmishes occur, there are good procedures to deal with them. The Chinese have never sent terrorists across or mistreated our soldiers, even in 1962.

It should now be clear that an alliance with China or an active confrontation with China will not be advantageous to us. We can continue to maintain the present uncertainties, sharing the Chinese view that the 'time is not ripe'. This is an acknowledgement that there is no political consensus in either country for a settlement of the question. This is a position of inertia and a counsel of despair.

All the arguments about the origin of the border are well known and there is little new that can be discovered. We have implicitly accepted that the border in the western sector is not established with precision by accepting a 'line of actual control'. If we choose inertia and move the time for a decision to an uncertain date in future, we will only be encouraging bigger and bigger defense budgets without necessarily adding to our security. The push for more weapon purchases and closer coordination with the US and its allies will also put us in the position of 'willing to wound, and yet afraid to strike', never able to take a military initiative, but be seen as antagonistic by China, a situation that only does grave disservice to our people.

Why not our political parties join together to study the possible contours of a peace settlement with China – play a 'peace game' on how to arrive at a settlement of the border problem similar to the military playing war games to assess the enemy and refine strategy? This is the 'game' in which political parties have to rise above limited electoral considerations to work for a consensus – not an unreasonable expectation because the major parties of our polity have contributed to the shaping of all the agreements between India and China since the 1980s and almost all other parties have been in one government or the other that signed these agreements. It will be presumptuous for one person to propose the contours of a consensus, but one can still attempt to indicate the themes that require a debate to arrive at a consensus.

Today, China is among our most important trade partners. This situation will remain and become stronger and multilateral links, like the BRICS and the Shanghai Cooperation Organisation add their weight to economic cooperation activities. It is not argued that trade per se will help peace between nations because past record on whether increase in trade will help increase the chance of peace between trade partners is murky at best. Trade restrictions and sanctions have also become war by other means these days. It is only meant here that the barriers that existed between the two countries have fallen to some extent and the number of people in both countries with an interest in a tranquil bilateral environment has become larger. Secondly, it goes without saying that if India wishes a very substantial increase in investments, China is one of the few obvious places to go. One goes to the bank because that is where the money is. China has more than $ 3 trillion in reserves and it would make sense for them to earn more money from it than what it earns by keeping on investing in the US Treasury securities. It is for us to make it worth their while to do so. Thirdly, it is essential that our public has a fair understanding of the status of the border. It is a happy sign that the 50th anniversary of the 1962 war was used by India for a sober discussion of the question rather than for any display of jingoism. Unlike on earlier occasions, the Chinese response to Prime Minister Modi, when he addressed the people of Arunachal Pradesh as Prime Minister candidate of his party, was limited to stating that China only wished good relations with India rather than rebutting his statements or attacking him. When both sides shed the doctrinaire positions, it should be possible to begin to identify on the ground and in practical terms the exact contours of the border. There are aspects of the border that engage the 'feelings of the people' of the two countries, a criterion accepted by both the parties as a relevant factor. What are the matters related to the border negotiations with China that deeply engage the 'feelings' of our people? Let us agree on them and shore them up as part of an amicable resolution.

This essay has argued how the deterioration of the situation in Tibet also contributed to the deterioration of India-China relations in the 1950s and contributed to the border conflict. We have accepted that Tibet is a part of China and do not have to repeat it on each occasion our leaders meet. There are profound cultural links between India and Tibet just as there is shared culture and person-to-person contact on a large scale with every one of our neighbours. If we can sustain such links while honouring the sovereignty of our other neighbours, there is no reason we cannot do it in Tibet. How to sustain and foster them without, in any way, amending our political position also requires a consensus within and in exchanges with China.

The texts of the most important agreements on the border question are attached at Appendices A to C. It will be useful for readers to study them and form their own ideas on how this challenge can be addressed most advantageously.

China has plenty of problems within just as we too have. China has never considered the Indian border as grave an issue as the South China Sea. Weiqi principles show that it would be beneficial for it to deal with the smaller faceoff, as it is compelled to deal with the larger ones on the other parts of its large and troublesome borders. Therefore, we need not assume that China would not, at all, be amenable to negotiations. We do not have to admire China, learn from China, show that we are friends or talk about age old ties. But we have to live as a neighbour with China. The settlement of the border dispute will produce the immediate effect of energising us in the conduct of our foreign policy, strengthening our hand in the relations with Pakistan, and reducing the burden on our army, which, in turn, will allow us to use our resources for the defence of our country and the greater welfare of our people in a much more effective manner. All these, we owe to our people.

Chapter XV

Some Concluding Remarks

While embarking on his epic narration of *Raghuvamsam*, even the immortal Kalidasa modestly asked, "Where is the dynasty that originates with the Sun and where is this person of little wisdom?" When the subject is the country with the grandest and most dramatic of histories among nations, the same question can be asked with even more apt modesty by this student of the subject. Yet, to continue with the simile used by Kalidasa to conclude his shloka, we have indeed crossed that ocean in this simple bark to arrive at the present from the mists of antiquity and to take a peep at the future.

Vast amount of literature on China engages itself with India 'catching up' with China or 'falling behind' it. This essay, hopefully, demonstrates that this is a matter we in India should not get obsessed with. Ever since the weakening of the Chinese Empire in the mid-19th century, the point of time from which modern Chinese measure their 'century of national humiliation', a strong China that could stand up to the world was what was sought by the intellectuals and political strategists. Military strength and economic power weighed high in their calculations. In the same period of history, since the failure of the 1857 uprising, our leaders and thinkers sought a social revolution as essential component of national liberation with an emphasis on equity and justice. It is pointless to debate which is better, whether to bend the entire energy of the society for its collective strength and suspend concern for individual well-being and choose the alternative because each arises from the innate nature of the individual society. This essay, one hopes, has also shown that the habits of the unitary administrative system and the closed nature of decision making that has become second nature in China through its use over thousands of years are unknown to us and is incapable of implementation in India because it is alien to our political and social DNA. Such a system is quick in decision making, but its errors are not easily discovered and quickly corrected as we have seen from the examples of the Great Leap Forward and the ensuing famine and the calamities ensuing from the arbitrarily imposed one child policy. Nor are major policy blunders judged and punished within reasonable timeframes. How many such wrong policies with possible disastrous consequences lurk in China at present, no one knows. Therefore, in the case of modern China, it may be said that it is the past rather than the future that is uncertain as facts about what actually transpired emerge decades later in the absence of an open press, a probing judiciary and an alert Parliament that is quickly punished for misreading the public mood.

We have also seen that China had unique advantages in the form of a readymade Hong Kong and, later, a similarly developed Taiwan. When China decided that confrontation with the USA was no longer a beneficial proposition, it made a huge strategic turnaround that helped both China and the USA. They helped each other in their separate confrontations with the Soviet Union. The specific context helped China in its program of opening up thanks to the benign political attitude of the USA, a situation not necessarily obtained by any other developing country. Thus, the favourable international political climate was as much a factor in China's rapid growth and the unique benefit of having a Hong Kong and a Taiwan offering infrastructure of the highest quality without paying for it as well as large investments and high technical skills from areas with similar cultural traditions – all of them conditions impossible to replicate for other countries.

The second theme of the unresolved border between India and China should also be seen in the larger Asian context. The possibilities of conflict generally increase with the number of countries with which a country shares borders. If we add maritime neighbours, China has more of them than any other country in the world, in addition to the existence of what it considers a rebel province of Taiwan. China settled the borders with most of its smaller neighbours long time back. It has not only resolved its border issues with Russia, which are extremely complex because of a bunch of islands in a large border river, but also developed flourishing economic exchanges. We have also seen that China has, for all practical purposes, abandoned the idea of using force to annex Taiwan. At the same time, problems between China and Japan have exacerbated; China has also declared that the ownership of the islands in the South China Sea is a 'core issue'. It is in this context that it is argued that we should make a concerted effort to arrive at a domestically agreed position about resolving the border question with China.

Leaving aside the question of the viability of a constant military confrontation with China, we should ponder how it restricts us diplomatically and economically. There is, therefore, force in the argument that there is space for both China and India in the future Asia. A better and clearer understanding of China will help the informed public opinion in India to judge the scope of this suggestion. This essay is an attempt to contribute to this important endeavour.

Notes

1. Arnold J. Toynbee, *A Study of History,* Abridgement of Volume I-VI by D.C. Somervell, (Oxford University Press, 1946), p. 1.

2. Amaury de, Riencourt, *The Soul of China,* (New York: Harper, 1965), p. 3.

3. The most detailed treatment of this subject could be found in C. P FitzGerald, *The Chinese View of their Place in the World,* (Oxford University Press, 1964).

4. An interesting treatment of the history, symbolism, and the current propaganda use of the Great Wall by the Chinese government may be found in Julia Lovell, *The Great Wall: China Against the World,* (New York: Grove Press, 2006).

5. Amaury de Riencourt, op. cit., pp. 24-25.

6. Etienne Balazs quoted in Ross Terrill, *The New Chinese Empire*, (New York: Basic Books, 2003), p. 52.

7. Amaury de Riencourt, op. cit., p. 25.

8. Ibid., pp. 6-7.

9. Ross Terrill, *The New Chinese Empire*, op. cit., pp. 50-52 discusses the socio-political and psychological impact of this unique script on Chinese people and the ruling system.

10. Bruce Gilley, *China's Democratic Future*, (New York: Colombia University Press, 2004).

11. Li Zhisui, *The Private Life of Chairman Mao*, (London: Random House, 1994).

12. Wang Hui, "New Criticism" in *One China, Many Paths*, (New York: Verso, 2003), p. 65.

13. Margaret McMillan, *Nixon and Mao* (New York: Random House, 2007), p. 269.

14. Statement by Hermann Keyserling, quoted by Amaury de Riencourt, op. cit, p. 105.

15. Jean C Oi, *State and Peasant in Contemporary China*, (Berkeley: University of California Press, , 1989), p. 48-9.

16. Li Changping, "Crisis in the Countryside" in *One China Many Paths*, op. cit.

17. Frank Dikotter, *Mao's Great Famine: The History of China's Most Devastating Catastrophe, 1958-1962* (New York: Walker & Co, 2010), p. 192.

18. Hu Angang, "Equity and Efficiency" in *One China, Many Paths*, op. cit.

19. Xi Chunying, Dy. Chairman of the Law Committee of the National People's Congress in an interview with Associated Press, June 29, 2007, cited in Susan L Shirk, *China: Fragile Superpower.*

20. Wang Yi, "From Status to Contract" in *One China, Many Paths*, op. cit. p. 192.

21. Philip P Pan, *Out of Mao's Shadow: The Struggle for the Soul of a New China*, (New York: Simon & Shuster, 2008), p. 165.

22. For a detailed discussion on growth and its constraints, see Will Hutton, *Writing on the Wall*, (New York: Free Press, 2006).

23. Details of trade surplus for some years recorded below will illustrate this point.

Year	Chinese Trade Surplus (US $) (Rounded to nearest billion)	Surplus with USA (US$)
2001	22 billion	83 billion
2002	30 billion	103 billion
2003	26 billion	124billion
2004	32billion	162 billon
2005	102billion	202 billion
2006	177 billion	232 billion
2007	261 billion	256 billion
2008	298 billion	266 billion
2009	196 billion	226 billion
2010	183 billion	181 billion
2011	155 billion	202 billion

24. He Qinglian, "A Listing Social Structure" in *One China, Many Paths,* op. cit.

25. "Trends and Risks of Changes in China's Social Structure in the near Future," *Strategy and Management*, Issue No. 5 of 1998.

26. C.P. FitzGerald, op. cit., p. 19.

27. Paper by Judith Banister et al, *Population and Development Review.* Volume 10, No. 2 of June 1984 and Volume 10, No. 4 (December 1984), respectively, cited by Frank Dikotter op. cit. Yang Jisheng Chinese, *Mubei: Zhongguo liushiniandai dajihuang jishi* (Wooden Tombcover: A True History of the

Great Famine in China in the Sixties), (Hong Kong, 2008).

28. Rob Gifford, *China Road,* (New York: Random House, 2007) pp. 180 -182. He narrates the story of the abortion doctor travelling in a bus and the other travellers caustically commenting on her work after she gets down. The comment on enforced abortion is on page 181.

29. Pan Yue, the Chinese Minister for Environment in an interview with *Der Spiegel,* April 2006.

30. Elizabeth Economy, *The River Runs Black,* (Ithaca, New York: Cornell University Press, 2004). It offers the most detailed picture of the way China has polluted its water, air and soil. Philip P. Pan, op. cit. also devotes an entire chapter to the very hazardous coal mining industry.

31. Giovanni Arrighi, *Adam Smith in Beijing*, (New York: Verso, 2007), p. 389.

32. Philip P. Pan, op. cit. p. 118.

33. Li Changping, "Crisis in the Countryside," op. cit.

34. Chinadigitaltimes.net/2005/08/regulations_on.pnp quoted in Ian Bremer, *The J Curve,* (New York: Simon & Schuster, 2006), p. 246.

35. Ye Hailin's article in *China Daily,* September 3, 2008.

36. Julia Lovell, *The Opium War*, (London: Picador, 2011), p. 344. She also cites the *People's Daily* quoted here.

37. Margaret MacMillan, op. cit., p. 234.

38. Will Hutton, op. cit. and Michael Lind in *Vietnam: The Necessary War*, (New York: Basic Books, 2001) argue cogently that the Vietnam War was ultimately a policy success for the USA, 'a remarkable unsung success for American policy' in 'a surrogate war against China' as Will Hutton puts it.

39. Ncholas D. Kristoff and Sheryl WuDunn, *China Wakes: The Struggle for the Soul of a Rising Power*, (New York: Random House, 1994), quoted on p. 304.

40. The various scenarios of China's transition to a different form of government form the subject of Minxin Pei's *China's Trapped Transition: The Limits of Developmental Autocracy*, (Harvard University Press, 2006).

Appendix A

Sino-Indian Joint Press Communique

1988/12/23

(Beijing, 23 December 1988)

At the invitation of Premier Li Peng of the State Council of the People's Republic of China, Prime Minister Rajiv Gandhi of the Republic of India made and official goodwill visit to the People's Republic of China from 19 to 23 December 1988. Accompanying His Excellency Prime Minister Rajiv Gandhi on his visit to China were Mrs. Sonia Gandhi, Mr. Narasimha Rao, Minister of External Affairs of India, Mr. Dinesh Singh, Minister of Commerce, Dr. B. Shankaranand, Minister of Law and Justice and Water Resources, Mr. K. Natwar Singh, Minister of State for External Affairs, and other Indian officials.

Premier Li Peng and Prime Minister Rajiv Gandhi held talks in an atmosphere of friendship, candidness and mutual understanding. President Yang Shangkun of the People's Republic of China, General secretary Zhao Ziyang of the Central Committee of the Communist Party of China (CPC) and Chairman Deng Xiaoping of the Military Commission of the CPC Central Committee had separate meetings with Prime Minister Rajiv Gandhi. During his visit, the two Governments signed the Agreement on Cooperation in the Field of Science and Technology, the agreement Relating to Civil Air Transport, and the Executive Programme for the Years 1988, 1988 and 1990 under the Agreement for Cultural Cooperation. Both the Premier and the Prime Minister were present at the signing ceremony. The Prime Minister Rajiv Gandhi, Mrs. Gandhi and their party also toured historical sites and scenic spots in Beijing, Xi'an and Shanghai.

During their talks and meetings, the leaders of the two countries had a wide exchange of views and ideas on bilateral relations and international issues of mutual interest. Both sides found such talks and meetings useful as they enhanced mutual understanding in the interest of further improvement and development of bilateral relations. The two sides made a positive appraisal of the cooperation and exchanges in recent years in trade, culture, science and technology, civil aviation and other fields, and expressed satisfaction with the relevant agreements reached between the two countries. They emphasized the vast scope that existed for learning from each other.

They emphasized that the Five Principles of mutual respect for sovereignty and territorial integrity, mutual non-aggression, non-interference in each other's internal affairs, equality and mutual benefit, and peaceful coexistence, which were jointly initiated by China and India and which have proved full of vitality through the test of history, constitute the basic guiding principles for good relations between states. These principles also constitute the basic guidelines for the establishment of a new international political order and the new international economic order. Both sides agreed that their common desire was to restore, improve and develop Sino-Indian good-neighborly and friendly relations on the basis of these principles. This not only conforms to the fundamental interests of the two peoples, but will actively contribute to peace and stability in Asia and the world as a whole. The two sides reaffirmed that they would make efforts to further their friendly relation.

The leaders of the two countries held earnest, indepth discussions on the Sino-Indian boundary question and agreed to settle this question through peaceful and friendly consultations. They also agreed to develop their relations actively in other fields and work hard to create a favourable climate and conditions for a fair and reasonable settlement of the boundary question while seeking a mutually acceptable solution to this question. In this context, concrete steps will be taken, such as establishing a joint working group on the boundary question and a joint group on economic relations and trade and science and technology.

The Chinese side expressed concern over anti-China activities by some Tibetan elements in India. The Indian side reiterated the long-standing and consistent policy of the Government of India that Tibet is an autonomous region of China and that anti-China political activities by Tibetan elements are not permitted on Indian soil.

With regard to the international situation, the two sides held that in the present-day world, confrontation was giving way to dialogue and tension to relaxation. This is a trend resulting from long years of unswerving struggle by the peace-loving countries and people of the world against power politics. It is conducive to world peace and to the settlement of regional problems. It also facilitates the efforts of all countries, the developing countries in particular, to develop their national economies. China and India will make their own contributions to the maintenance of world peace, promotion of complete disarmament and attainment of common progress.

His Excellency Prime minister Rajiv Gandhi, Mrs. Sonia Gandhi and their party expressed heartfelt thanks to the Government and people of the People's Republic of China for the warm and friendly hospitality accorded them.

Prime Minister Rajiv Gandhi has invited Premier Li Peng to visit the Republic of India at his convenience. Premier Li Peng has accepted the invitation with pleasure. And the date of the visit will be decided upon through diplomatic channnels.

(http://in.china-embassy.org/eng/zygxc/wx/t762866.htm)

Appendix B

Agreement on The Maintenance of Peace Along The Line of Actual Control in The India-China Border

SEPTEMBER 7, 1993

The Government of the Republic of India and the Government of the People's Republic of China (hereinafter referred to as the two sides), have entered into the present Agreement in accordance with the Five Principles of mutual respect for sovereignty and territorial integrity, mutual non-aggression, non-interference in each other's internal affairs, equality and mutual benefit and peaceful coexistence and with a view to maintaining peace and tranquility in areas along the line of actual control in the India-China border areas.

1. The two sides are of the view that the India-China boundary question shall be resolved through peaceful and friendly consultations. Neither side shall use or threaten to use force against the other by any means. Pending an ultimate solution to the boundary question between the two countries, the two sides shall strictly respect and observe the line of actual control between the two sides. No activities of either side shall overstep the line of actual control. In case personnel of one side cross the line of actual control, upon being cautioned by the other side, they shall immediately pull back to their own side of the line of actual control. When necessary, the two sides shall jointly check and determine the segments of the line of actual control where they have different views as to its alignment.

2. Each side will keep its military forces in the areas along the line of actual control to a minimum level compatible with

the friendly and good neighbourly relations between the two countries. The two sides agree to reduce their military forces along the line of actual control in conformity with the requirements of the principle of mutual and equal security to ceilings to be mutually agreed. The extent, depth, timing, and nature of reduction of military forces along the line of actual control shall be determined through mutual consultations between the two countries. The reduction of military forces shall be carried out by stages in mutually agreed geographical locations sector-wise within the areas along the line of actual control.

3. Both sides shall work out through consultations effective confidence building measures in the areas along the line of actual control. Neither side will undertake specified levels of military exercises in mutually identified zones. Each side shall give the other prior notification of military exercises of specified levels near the line of actual control permitted under this Agreement.

4. In case of contingencies or other problems arising in the areas along the line of actual control, the two sides shall deal with them through meetings and friendly consultations between border personnel of the two countries. The form of such meetings and channels of communications between the border personnel shall be mutually agreed upon by the two sides.

5. The two sides agree to take adequate measures to ensure that air intrusions across the line of actual control do not take place and shall undertake mutual consultations should intrusions occur. Both sides shall also consult on possible restrictions on air exercises in areas to be mutually agreed near the line of actual control.

6. The two sides agree that references to the line of actual control in this Agreement do not prejudice their respective positions on the boundary question.

7. The two sides shall agree through consultations on the form, method, scale and content of effective verification measures and supervision required for the reduction of military forces and the maintenance of peace and tranquility in the areas along the line of actual control under this Agreement.

8. Each side of the India-China Joint Working Group on the boundary question shall appoint diplomatic and military experts to formulate, through mutual consultations, implementation measures for the present Agreement. The experts shall advise the Joint Working Group on the resolution of differences between the two sides on the alignment of the line of actual control and address issues relating to redeployment with a view to reduction of military forces in the areas along the line of actual control. The experts shall also assist the Joint Working Group in supervision of the implementation of the Agreement, and settlement of differences that may arise in that process, based on the principle of good faith and mutual confidence.

9. The present Agreement shall come into effect as of the date of signature and is subject to amendment and addition by agreement of the two sides.

Signed in duplicate at Beijing on the Seventh day of September 1993 in the Hindi, Chinese and English languages, all three texts having equal validity.

[Signed:]

R. L. Bhatia
Minister of State for External Affairs
Republic of India

Tang Jiaxuan
Vice-Foreign Minister
People›s Republic of China

Source: (http://www.stimson.org/research-pages/agreement-on-the-maintenance-of-peace-along-the-line-of-actual-control-in-the-india-china-border/)

Appendic C

Declaration on Principles for Relations and Comprehensive Cooperation Between the Republic of India and the People's Republic of China

June 23, 2003

At the invitation of Premier of the State Council of the People's Republic of China H.E. Wen Jiabao, Prime Minister of the Republic of India H.E. Atal Bihari Vajpayee paid an official visit to the People's Republic of China from 22 to 27 June 2003.

During this visit, Premier Wen Jiabao held talks with Prime Minister Vajpayee. Their Excellencies President Hu Jintao of the People's Republic of China, Chairman Jiang Zemin of the Central Military Commission, Chairman Wu Bangguo of the Standing Committee of the National People's Congress and Vice President Zeng Qinghong of the People's Republic of China held separate meetings with Prime Minister Vajpayee. The talks and meetings were held in a sincere and friendly atmosphere.

Leaders from both countries noted with satisfaction the progress made over recent years in bilateral relations. This is conducive not only to their respective development, but also to regional stability and prosperity. The two sides recalled the historical depth of their friendly contacts. India and China are the two largest developing countries of the world with centuries-old civilization, unique history and similar objectives. Both noted that the sustained economic and social development in the two countries, representing one third of humanity is vital for ensuring peace, stability and prosperity not only in Asia but also in the whole world.

The two sides agreed that India and China have a mutual desire for good neighbourly relations and have broad common interests. They agreed to fully utilize the substantial potential and opportunities for deepening mutually beneficial cooperation.

Friendship and cooperation between the two countries meets the need to:

1. promote the socio-economic development and prosperity of both India and China;
2. maintain peace and stability regionally and globally;
3. strengthen multipolarity at the international level; and
4. enhance the positive factors of globalization.

Both sides affirmed that they would abide by the following principles, promote a long-term constructive and cooperative partnership and, on this basis, build a qualitatively new relationship:

1. Both sides are committed to developing their long-term constructive and cooperative partnership on the basis of the principles of Panchsheel, mutual respect and sensitivity for each other's concerns and equality;
2. As two major developing countries, India and China have a broad mutual interest in the maintenance of peace, stability and prosperity in Asia and the world, and a mutual desire in developing wider and closer cooperation and understanding in regional and international affairs;
3. The common interests of the two sides outweigh their differences. The two countries are not a threat to each other. Neither side shall use or threaten to use force against the other; and
4. Both sides agree to qualitatively enhancing the bilateral relationship at all levels and in all areas while addressing differences through peaceful means in a fair, reasonable and mutually acceptable manner. The differences should not be allowed to affect the overall development of bilateral relations.

Both sides agreed to hold regular high-level exchanges between the two countries. This will greatly enhance mutual understanding and expand bilateral relations. With a view to deepening their coordination and dialogues on bilateral, regional and international issues, both sides agreed on the need for annual meetings between Foreign Ministers of the two countries. They also agreed that personnel exchanges and friendly contacts between ministries, parliaments and political parties of the two countries should be further enhanced.

The two sides welcomed the positive momentum of bilateral trade and economic cooperation in recent years and shared the belief that continued expansion and intensification of India-China economic cooperation is essential for strengthening bilateral relations.

Both sides shared the view that existing complementarities between their two economies provide an important foundation and offer broad prospects for further enhancing their economic relations. In order to promote trade and economic cooperation, both sides will take necessary measures consistent with their national laws and rules and international obligations to remove impediments to bilateral trade and investment. They reaffirmed the importance of the ministerial meeting of the Joint Economic Group (JEG) and agreed to hold the next (seventh) JEG meeting within the year.

The two sides will set up a compact Joint Study Group (JSG) composed of officials and economists to examine the potential complementarities between the two countries in expanded trade and economic cooperation. The JSG would also draw up a programme for the development of India-China trade and economic cooperation for the next five years, aimed at encouraging greater cooperation between the business communities of both sides. The Group should present a study report and recommendations to the two Governments on measures for comprehensive trade and economic cooperation by the end of June 2004.

The two countries will launch a financial dialogue and cooperation mechanism to strengthen their dialogue and coordination in this sector.

The two sides agreed to enhance cooperation at the World Trade Organization, which is not only to mutual benefit but also in the broader interest of developing countries. The two sides will hold dialogues on a regular basis in this regard.

Historical and cultural links between India and China will be strengthened, inter-alia, through the promotion of exchanges in culture, education, science and technology, media, youth and people-to-people relations. They agreed to set up Cultural Centers in each other›s capitals and facilitate their establishment.

Both sides will work towards the enhancement of direct air and shipping links, tourism, exchange hydrological data in flood season on common rivers as agreed, cooperation in agriculture, dairy, food processing, health and other sectors.

They agreed on the need to broaden and deepen defence exchanges between the two countries, which will help enhance and deepen the mutual understanding and trust between the two armed forces. They confirmed that the exchange of visits by their Defence Ministers and of military officials at various levels should be strengthened.

The two sides exchanged views on the India-China boundary question and expounded their respective positions. They reiterated their readiness to seek a fair, reasonable and mutually acceptable solution through consultations on an equal footing. The two sides agreed that pending an ultimate solution, they should work together to maintain peace and tranquillity in the border areas, and reiterated their commitment to continue implementation of the agreements signed for this purpose, including the clarification of the Line of Actual Control.

The two sides agreed to each appoint a Special Representative to explore from the political perspective of the overall bilateral relationship the framework of a boundary settlement.

The Indian side recognizes that the Tibet Autonomous Region is part of the territory of the People›s Republic of China and reiterates that it does not allow Tibetans to engage in anti-China political activities in India. The Chinese side expresses its appreciation for the Indian position and reiterates that it is firmly opposed to any attempt and action aimed at splitting China and bringing about «independence of Tibet".

The Indian side recalled that India was among the first countries to recognize that there is one China and its one China policy remains unaltered. The Chinese side expressed its appreciation of the Indian position.

India and China recognized the primacy of maintaining international peace. This is a prerequisite for the socio-economic development of all developing countries, including India and China. The world is marked by diversity. Every country has the right to choose its own political system and path to development. As two major developing countries, India and China acknowledged the importance of their respective roles in the shaping of a new international political and economic order. The international community must help the developing countries to eliminate poverty and narrow the gap between the North and the South through dialogue and cooperation so as to achieve common prosperity.

The two sides acknowledged the vital importance of the role of the United Nations in world peace, stability and development. They are determined to continue their efforts in strengthening the UN system. They reaffirmed their readiness to work together to promote reform of the UN. In reform of the UN Security Council, priority should be given to enhancing representation of the developing countries.

Both sides stood for continued multilateral arms control and disarmament process, undiminished and equal security for all at progressively lower levels of armament and for multilateral negotiations aimed at nuclear disarmament and elimination of nuclear weapons. They are firmly opposed to introduction of weapons in outer space, use or threat of force against space-based objects and support cooperation in development of space technology for peaceful purposes.

The two sides recognised the threat posed by terrorism to them and to global peace and security. They resolutely condemned terrorism in any form. The struggle between the international community and global terrorism is a comprehensive and sustained one, with the ultimate objective of eradication of terrorism in all regions. This requires strengthening the global legal framework against terrorism. Both sides shall also promote cooperation on counter-terrorism through their bilateral dialogue mechanism.

India and China face special and similar challenges in their efforts to protect the environment while simultaneously forging ahead with rapid social and economic development of their countries. In this context, the two sides agreed to work together in a practical manner to cooperate on preserving the environment and ensuring sustainable development and to coordinate positions on climate change, biodiversity and other issues in relevant multilateral fora.

The two sides supported multilateral cooperation in Asia, believing that such cooperation promotes mutually beneficial exchanges, economic growth as well as greater cohesion among Asian countries. The two sides viewed positively each other›s participation in regional and sub-regional multilateral cooperation processes in Asia.

The two sides stated that the improvement and development of India-China relations is not targeted at any third country and does not affect either country›s existing friendly relations and cooperation with other countries.

The two sides agreed that the official visit of the Prime Minister of India to the People›s Republic of China has been a success, has contributed to enhancing mutual understanding and trust between the Governments, leaders and peoples of the two countries, and marks a new step forward in strengthening the all-round cooperation between India and China in the new century.

Prime Minister Vajpayee invited Premier Wen Jiabao to visit India at a mutually convenient time and conveyed to President Hu Jintao an invitation from President Abdul Kalam to visit India. The Chinese side accepted the invitations with appreciation. The dates of the visits will be settled through diplomatic channels. On behalf of the Government and the people of India, H.E Prime Minister Atal Bihari Vajpayee thanked the Government and the people of China for the warm welcome received by him and his delegation.

Signed in Beijing on 23 June 2003 in the Hindi, Chinese and English languages.

(Atal Bihari Vajpayee)	(Wen Jiabao)
Prime Minister	Premier of the State Council
The Republic of India	The People's Republic of China

Source: (http://www.mea.gov.in/in-focus-article.htm?7679/Declaration+on+Principles+for+Relations+and+Comprehensive+Cooperation+Between+the+Republic+of+India+and+the+Peoples+Republic+of+China)

Index

O

P

Q

R

S

Y

Z

www.ingramcontent.com/pod-product-compliance
Lightning Source LLC
Chambersburg PA
CBHW031136270326
41929CB00011B/1641

* 9 7 8 9 3 8 5 5 6 3 0 4 1 *